PENGUIN BO
WOMEN OF INFLUENCE

Rajni Sekhri Sibal is a writer and an IAS officer. She topped the civil services examination in 1986 and was Secretary, Government of India. Rajni has worked in various capacities handling programme implementation and policymaking at the state as well as the national level. She is the recipient of the Indian of the Year Award in the category 'Unsung Hero'.

She has authored *Cloud's End and Beyond*, *Kamadhenu*, *Are You Prepared for a Disaster?*, *Fragrant Words*, *The Haunting Himalayas* and *Asariri*. *Women of Influence* is her seventh book.

WOMEN
OF
INFLUENCE

TEN EXTRAORDINARY
IAS CAREERS

RAJNI SEKHRI SIBAL

PENGUIN BOOKS

An imprint of Penguin Random House

PENGUIN BOOKS

USA | Canada | UK | Ireland | Australia
New Zealand | India | South Africa | China

Penguin Books is part of the Penguin Random House group of companies
whose addresses can be found at global.penguinrandomhouse.com

Published by Penguin Random House India Pvt. Ltd
4th Floor, Capital Tower 1, MG Road,
Gurugram 122 002, Haryana, India

Penguin
Random House
India

First published in Penguin Books by Penguin Random House India 2021

ISBN 9780143454069

Typeset in Adobe Garamond Pro by Manipal Technologies Limited, Manipal
Printed at Thomson Press India Ltd, New Delhi

www.penguin.co.in

MIX
Paper
FSC FSC® C010615

When you walk along a path that's narrow and straight,
and a storm tries to blow you astray,
then with a resolute spirit, hold your head up high,
and with a stride that's firm, push the doubts away.

When you stand for a cause that's lofty and true,
stand tall like a tree in the rain,
if the wind is strong and you fall to the ground,
sprout like an acorn and grow tall again.

For all the officers and women of influence this book is about and for all the inspiring people out there

. . . and to my eternal sources of inspiration, Lakshi and Pushan

Contents

Author's Note

I have often wondered why some stories do not get told . . .

It is true that civil servants form the steel framework of the administrative system in India, the negative connotations of the word 'Babu' used commonly by the media notwithstanding. The All-India Civil Services Examination, conducted by the Union Public Service Commission (UPSC), is arguably one of the most competitive examinations in India. Every year, between 80,00,00 and 10,00,000 bright young aspirants compete for several hundred posts in the civil services. Except for when a candidate excels in the entrance exam, and is briefly in the spotlight, very little is known about their work or the life they lead. Several autobiographies and a few biographies of officers are in the public domain. Most of what has been published so far is about the contributions of a few male civil servants. The stories of *women* of influence, in the civil services, remain untold.

Women of Influence is a compilation of hitherto untold stories of ten empowered civil servants—inspiring women who have walked that extra mile and made a difference. This book is *not* a statement on gender or an attempt at establishing one-upmanship. Having worked with many inspirational women and men, I am convinced that there is no basis for accepting any possible gender-based distinction. I firmly believe gender has absolutely nothing to do with one's efficiency or effectiveness. Some day, I hope to be able to share inspiring memoirs of some of my extraordinary male colleagues too.

At the very outset, I also need to state that besides the ten women portrayed in this book, there are many remarkable civil servants in the Indian Police, Foreign Service, Revenue and Forest Services; in Railways, Customs, Audit and Accounts, and other civil services. Similarly, there are many other outstanding women in the Indian Administrative Service (IAS). Perhaps I will relate the fascinating accounts of some other exceptional officers from all the different branches in a sequel to this book.

For the present, this book, *Women of Influence*, is about ten extraordinary women in the IAS, who have done some brilliant work under intense pressure and in adverse circumstances. The protagonists in this book are representative of a larger set of dynamic civil servants working against all odds.

Every woman of influence in my book is bright, focused, courageous, and has worked diligently over and above the call of duty. However, to say that she is remarkable doesn't mean that she is a paragon of virtue at all times. So, she may have performed exceptionally well in the episode related in the book, but may not have been brilliant at other times in different circumstances.

Grapevines often play a crucial role in such judgements. One criticizes another with a coloured perspective, and according to one's own—often skewed—life experiences. Grapevines, in any case, are personal opinions and rather tiresome.

As the author of the book, I do not want to put my heroines on a pedestal. It is not my intention to portray that the protagonists in the book are perfect. No one is. Nor do I proclaim that they have no flaws. Every human being has something good in them, along with some imperfections. I am merely presenting those positive episodes in the careers of these ten women, which are worth recounting.

In the events narrated in the book, each of my heroines has displayed incredible strength of character. The book tells stories about real-life experiences. However, I have taken the author's liberty to embellish the stories with some fringe anecdotes and conversations, even as the core stays genuine and intact.

The experiences reported in this book are disparate, and the genre of the stories distinct. The central characters belong to different generations. The narratives refer to events that occurred during different time periods and across diverse geographies. Some of the pieces are episodic and take the reader through events in which the protagonist displayed exemplary courage under difficult circumstances, or stood her ground and showed leadership qualities that helped diffuse a potentially catastrophic situation. Other stories present a period in the career of the protagonist that brings out her conviction and strategic thinking reflected in her policies. A few chapters describe longer journeys, where the protagonist's strategy included a plan and a process map that made all the difference.

Yet another category depicts the manner in which an idea became a movement, and how the intervention of a policy had a wider and more enduring impact—often one that proved to be path-breaking over the years. Each protagonist is an unsung hero in her own right.

All the central characters in the book belong to different age groups, batches, and cadres. They have different interests and varied academic and family backgrounds. Each has a unique personality. All ten of them differ in terms of what drives them. And yet, there is a common thread that binds them all: all of them have high ethical standards of integrity and all are bright, diligent, committed and courageous.

The facts and episodes were obtained from the protagonists themselves, or their close associates, or from unrelated people who had been affected. Some of the stories were further corroborated by newspaper reports. In one instance, where the protagonist was not in perfect health, the essential details were provided by her daughter who herself is a civil servant and currently works with the World Bank.

In another case, where the central character has passed away, the documented accounts of her work were complemented and completed by her friends, her son, and her husband—a civil servant and her batch mate. Their memories of the departed officer, and her work, helped to fill the gaps and also provided valuable information about her persona.

'Winds of Change', the opening story, is a chronicle of the first Indian woman to be appointed as Collector in a remote district in the Thar Desert, along the Indo-Pak border in Rajasthan, just before the 1965 War broke out. The times were ruled by conservative thinking. The district, in which the women wore long *ghoonghats*, took time to accept a woman as a Collector. The story details the journey of Otima's acceptance by the administration and the residents of the district. During those days, women did not work outside the home. She was the lone woman in her entire office and across all the offices in the district. The story reveals the commitment and persistent efforts of a wise and far-sighted Collector. Even as the desert sky was overcast with the clouds of war, she came to command respect from the patriarchal society through sheer grit and courage.

'Saving Lives' is the saga of India's victory over polio—a deadly disease that plagued the country for decades. Polio brought havoc in the lives of millions of children, causing acute flaccid paralysis of the limbs—and leaving them with lifelong debilitation for which there was no cure. The end of the country's battle against it was nowhere in sight, until Anuradha joined the Health Ministry and looked at the problem from an entirely different perspective. Her out-of-the-box thinking, and strategy, went a long way in attaining a sudden turnaround and taking the country over the finishing line. India reported its last case of wild polio in January 2011, and continues to be polio free.

'Power of the People' is a narrative about the commitment of an officer, who had unshakeable faith in the power of ordinary people to bring about momentous change in their own lives and in the lives of those around them. Anita was an activist and a bureaucrat. She threw hierarchy to the winds and put her trust in collaborations and in joining hands. An ardent believer in the efficacy of education, she was convinced that education was 'an effective tool to liberate all human beings from ignorance, prejudices, discrimination, hatred, and mindless violence'. The story follows her journey as she worked relentlessly, knowing full well that her effort would, in all probability, go unnoticed except by those for whom it was intended—the children. That was her sole reward and it was sufficient.

'Death in Police Custody' portrays the leadership qualities of a young officer, who managed a difficult situation that could have resulted in disturbing law and order, or in violence, but for her sensitivity and insight. She handled the situation deftly, preventing it from flaring up into a full-scale riot after a leader died in police custody. The officer displayed great fortitude. Despite being new to the post and the area, she took timely decisions with immense courage.

'Development amid Red Violence' is set in Chandrapur in the 1980s. Working in a Naxal-prone area had peculiar challenges. There was a genuine threat to the lives of those in the administration. Even though it would have been prudent to follow the security protocol, Malini, the protagonist, found it imperative for her to talk to the villagers and the tribals without her security personnel in tow. Their presence, essential for her personal safety, would intimidate the locals. Malini learnt to maintain a fine balance, which helped her build a rapport with the people. The story brings out her commitment and courage in the face of adversity.

'Sand in the Eye' is a story of a Subdivisional Magistrate, who had strong values inculcated in her by her middle-class family. She was a young and bold girl, faced with challenges from a notorious sand mafia. Times were tough, and she had little support in her endeavours to stop the illegal sand mining, merely a few kilometres away from the nation's capital . . . only a few years ago! The system found ways of removing the inconvenient officer and pushing her to the wall. Despite the strain, Durga did not succumb to intimidation and made a major dent in the unlawful practice.

'Computers and Viruses' gives us an insight into the management skills of the protagonist as she tries to introduce new technology in an organization. Change management is always a challenging task. The story relates the manner in which computerization was introduced into a public enterprise. There was great resistance to the introduction of computers from various quarters, in the early 1990s, as it happens with every change. Anita dealt with the resistance skillfully, ensuring a smooth and lasting transition.

'Kanooni Bibi and the Panchayat Elections' is an episodic narrative set in a border district of Punjab during the tumultuous 1980s. Its fulcrum is the efficacy of decision-making without fear or favour. Anjali was confronted with an unusual situation that had not been anticipated while framing the election rules. The challenge was to come up with a solution in a short time, one that could stand the test of time and judicial scrutiny—and also meet the criteria of equality and fairness. Kanooni, as an epithet, can mean over-scrupulous. However, the name Kanooni Bibi was conferred upon Anjali due to her uprightness, which endeared the Returning Officer to the electorate during the Panchayat Elections.

'Of Sensitive Sensibilities' chronicles the life of a protagonist, who was both sensitive and courageous. She took the lead in combating a scourge in our society—human trafficking. The narrative records the officer's battle against human trafficking in all its forms for the duration of her career. Bhamathi worked for the rehabilitation of trafficked victims wherever she was posted—and went through the entire gamut of research, advocacy, project implementation, and policy formulation.

'Flowering Success in the Land of the Rising Sun' is the story of a Chief Secretary, who never gave up on her dreams. She was undeterred by the problems of administering a beautiful but remote state in the north-east, and by its difficult terrain and inaccessibility. The complexities were compounded by the fact that the state had twenty-six major tribes and more than a100 subtribes, each with its unique characteristics. The account describes how strategic planning, and an imaginative and a purposeful approach to take the stakeholders along, guided Shakuntala in her journey in Arunachal Pradesh—the Land of the Rising Sun in India.

The Indian Administrative Service is indeed a dream career, but one that comes with great responsibility and the concomitant pressure. Having served in various positions in the IAS for the last three and a half decades, I am convinced that the Service provides one with a huge canvas and several opportunities to make changes in the lives you touch along the way.

A civil servant is at the helm of affairs at a very young age. After a rather comprehensive two-year training in governance, the selected officers of the Indian Administrative Service are posted in rural and semi-urban districts across India. They adapt to the environment, and adopt the culture of the cadre they are allotted. I am charmed when I see a Sikh colleague, who speaks impeccable Tamil, decide to build his own home in a state he had never visited before he was allotted the cadre; or when a person from Kerala is mistaken for a Bengali because he eats 'hilsa' like a pucca Bengali and sings 'Rabindra Sangeet as it should be sung!'

The first decade and a half in the IAS is spent in the field—in villages and small towns. One is the head of an entire subdivision in one's early twenties. There are challenges and opportunities as you handle sensitive matters in your very first posting. The Service provides the ability and the means for you to reach out and make a difference to the lives of the poorest of the poor, to listen to those whose voices are never heard, and to give succor to those who have no hope.

One plays multifarious roles, and the responsibility is extensive. The go-to person for just about everything on the ground is the Collector, Deputy Commissioner or District Magistrate—different designations assigned to the same person, depending upon the part of the country. The roles and responsibilities given to the Collector at the district level are, inter alia, performed by the Subdivisional Magistrate or SDM in a subdivision. Later, an IAS officer occupies more senior posts in the state and the government, and helps frame policies that impact different sectors in the state and across the entire country. The responsibility is vast as are the opportunities. There is no room for complacency.

The variety of sectors an IAS officer works in during her career takes her on an exciting voyage of constant learning.

She is on a steep learning curve and perpetually on her feet. The need and the opportunity to learn and to grow, is enormous. It is like a trek in the Himalayas. Once she reaches the summit after an arduous climb, she can't just sit back. She has to look ahead as she discovers yet another magnificent peak calling out to her. The ability to carry the skills and lessons from one area to another is a vital trait.

An officer may sometimes walk ten meaningful but entirely different paths in one lifetime. She could be putting together the budget for a state government one day, and heading an export-promotion corporation the next. A few years later, she could be responsible for formulating a pan-India policy for a green environment. To make significant contribution, she has to have her wits about her, coupled with a keen desire to learn. The journey is exhilarating and enriching.

Some of the strain is physical, while the other may be emotional or psychological. Let me mention two instances of the former kind following from the stories in the book: the first is that during an election, a Deputy Commissioner may not find any time to sleep for three days in a row; the second is that a Subdivisional Magistrate may have to face an angry crowd, and conduct an inquest into a death in police custody, despite running high fever. Each officer learns to deal with the pressure in her own manner.

This brings to mind the words *'ultima forsan'*—perhaps 'the final hour'. It has been a mantra for me (as much as Tagore's '*Ekla Chalo*') throughout my career, and has given me massive support. In the IAS one has no idea—and no control over—when and where one will be posted. So 'ultima forsan' works wonders in ensuring one does what is right and withstands the pressure. Whenever the choices were difficult—say, in a court matter, or on a file, these words were the guiding light. They provided clarity to the decision I took: 'If this is the last file I do in this office, or the last court order I handle in this district, how should I decide it?'

An officer can be transferred as many as four times in a year. In a field posting, she soon learns to live out of a suitcase—ready to shut its lid and go wherever she is posted. Every move entails a disruption in her family's life. For a young child, an interrupted academic year could mean changing eleven different schools by the time she enters class eight. And then there are always terrifying threats for a civil servant: a damaging appraisal, a negative verbal report that hinders empanelment, the possibility of a charge sheet to prevent a promotion, an arbitrary suspension order, and more.

Work–life balance in the civil services is particularly challenging for women, more so during field postings when the children are young. The job is gruelling and often demands one's attention night and day—as do the infants and children. So, an officer has to walk the tightrope rope between work pressure and the needs of her children. I have been frantically called out of an important meeting with a Chief Minister because my four-year-old son fell off a tree and broke his arm while plucking mangoes. In order to spend more time with the young ones, several lady officers take them along on tours. So, while I did my *girdawari* inspection of agricultural crops in the farmers' fields, my children had the sheer pleasure of running around in mustard-and-channa (gram) fields and riding a camel cart with all the other children in the village.

However, there is a flip side to these cheerful memories. An officer's affection for her family can sometimes be used as a pressure tactic by criminals and such. Sinister threats of *'Bacche uttha ke le jaayenge'*—roughly translated as 'We'll snatch your children', to influence an officer—have been dealt with on more than one occasion.

Yet, despite the pressure and stress inherent in the system, all civil servants leave a mark in some sphere or the other at some point in their careers. Several have shown exemplary courage and determination under difficult circumstances. Some have led teams that have helped build institutions. Others have been responsible for framing policies that made an enduring impact in various sectors. And still others have worked in situations that required strategic planning and an urgent solution.

Writing *Women of Influence* was a delightful learning experience for me. Over the last few months, the protagonists and I have started referring to this book as 'our book'. Working on this book has given me deep insight into the persona of many beautiful women and officers that I knew earlier only from afar. After writing each story, I would share it with the group—and the process brought us closer.

Most of the women I worked with and spoke to, while putting this book together, were rather reticent and had to be cajoled to talk about themselves. All of them preferred to talk about their work, their experiences, the problems along the way, and the processes they adopted to arrive at solutions, rather than their personal attributes. The book does not dwell upon their personality traits. However, as the narratives unfold, it becomes evident that the qualities the officer brought to the situation and her workplace made all the difference! That is even more reason why this book needed to be written.

As you read, you will find that none of the protagonists in this book fit the popular image of a 'Babu' sitting at her desk, merely whiling away the time and playing merry-go-round with dusty files and tangled red tape. Nor are they the archetypal stuffed shirts with a nose-in-the-air attitude. None of them have even a hint of spinelessness that Indian bureaucrats are believed to have. Nor do they quite fit the image of self-centered and self-serving people or gatekeepers, opposed to fresh ideas. None of them succumbed to any pressure, or allowed the surrounding dangers to affect their work.

Women of influence are in fact bright, committed, and hard-working. They work relentlessly at attaining their respective goals. They are open-minded and participatory in their approach. They believe in the rule of law and are firm believers in transparency. As you read the memoirs, you will find that despite dangerous situations quite often, they showed commendable spirit and leadership qualities. An element of conviction, commitment, and courage, runs across all the chapters in 'our book'.

I

Winds of Change

Desert sands under a scorching sun
and a time to defy the winds of war . . .

'Where is the border?' Otima had asked on that that fateful
night in 1965.

'Look, sa'ab. There are men from the other side behind
those sand dunes. See those silver edges over the horizon—
jahaan taare milte hain [where the earth and the sky meet]?'
Surja Ramji, the driver of the official car of the Collector of
Bikaner, replied pointing westwards.

Otima was surprised to hear Surja Ramji tell her that the
sand dunes behind which the enemy was located *became* the
border. She smiled as she recalled her response to her driver in
the Thar Desert that night. 'Amazing! A border that changes
with the wind. So every time a sand dune moves, the border
shifts, huh?'

The year 1965 is best remembered for the Indo-Pak War.
It was also the year when Bikaner got a Collector and District

Magistrate who was a woman. The fact was of historical significance. Rajasthan had never had a woman Collector before. The town of Bikaner was in a bit of a shock.

'How can we have a thirty-two-year-old *Bengali woman* as the Collector!'

'Ameeta? Or Omeeta?' asked someone in Bara Bazar, the old marketplace.

'No, no, her name is Otima. But what in the world does that mean?' said another.

'Uttama,' said a wise old man. 'Must be Uttama!'

In April 1965, when Otima started working as the Collector, Bikaner was a sleepy, conservative town with a population of less than 2,00,000 people. At that time, the district of Bikaner covered an area of 10,561 square miles and was sparsely populated with only 4,44,515 persons, as per the 1961 census, and had Bikaner town as its headquarters. From its small origins, the town has now become the fourth-largest city in Rajasthan. Today, the word 'Bikaner' is synonymous with 'Bikaneri Sweets' and 'Bikaneri Bhujiya'—a savoury made with chickpea flour—across India and amongst Indian diaspora all over the world.

Formerly the capital of the princely state of Bikaner, Bikaner town was founded by Rao Bika, a Rajput chieftain of the Rathor clan, in 1465. Before that it was a barren land called Jangaldesh. Since it was situated in the middle of the Thar Desert, Bikaner was also known as *registaan*—a desert land. The last Maharaja, Lieutenant-General Sir Sadul Singh, ceded his state to the Union of India in 1949.

The proud Rajput rulers of the erstwhile princely state continued to hold sway over society when Otima arrived in 1965. The Royal Family lived in Lalgarh Palace and commanded both respect and influence. Patriarchy was valued across Rajasthan, especially in its princely states. Women had limited voice in public, and most lived behind ghoonghats—a veil covering their faces almost down to their waists. *How could a woman lead a district?*—was the general refrain.

The people were dismayed, especially with the winds of war on the horizon. A woman as '*mai baap*' was unheard of in the male-dominated society. How could a non-Rajasthani female Collector ever understand the culture and needs of Bikaner *ki janata* [the people of Bikaner]? The Bengali city girl who grew up in Allahabad had an entirely different societal background! There was a rumour that the new Collector did not even speak good Hindi.

The only extenuating factor was that she was married to a Rajasthani—Anil Bordia, her batchmate. He had recently been posted to Bikaner as the new Additional Director, Education—a job he had chosen since he was passionate about education.

'Why couldn't they have put Bordia Sa'ab at the helm of affairs?' asked the *daroga* of Kote Gate.

'Why has he been given a relatively less prestigious job?' wondered a local politician.

The main concern of the staff at the Collectorate, Otima's office, was different.

'How do we address her? Sir? *Hukum*? Sa'ab? Collector Sa'ab? What?'

'How could this government give her collector-ship before offering it to her husband? And that too when he is such a good and bright Rajasthani boy!'—ran the general sentiment.

Otima was excited by the new challenge; she loved to plunge into the unknown. While all her batchmates were in the field, she had spent four years behind a desk in Jaipur, as a junior Deputy Secretary. The secretariat posting had suited her at that time as a soft landing into a new cadre. It also suited her as the mother of an infant. With her little daughter now being able to toddle around on her own, Otima was ready for a field posting. She was very excited on being the first woman to become a District Magistrate in Rajasthan—and she was raring to go!

The fact that she knew nothing about Bikaner district, except that it was on the Indo-Pak border in the Thar Desert, made no difference. The hot desert climate with very little rainfall and extreme temperatures did not deter her. She was delighted by the place, well aware that the summer temperatures could exceed 48°C, and during the winter they could dip well below freezing point.

The Collector's Residence, her new home, was gigantic and beautiful. The thick walls and the extraordinarily high ceilings were built for the desert. The house was ancient and full of cobwebs and piles of dust, despite the fact that it had been cleaned and painted for the new 'Collector Sa'ab'. Creaky antique fans blew hot air, and there was constant fear of strange insects and reptiles lurking in some nook or cranny.

Anil, her husband, could not care less about the reptiles and creepy-crawlies or even the vultures that abounded at their new place. He was thrilled with the outhouse that would become his home-office. Maitreyi, their daughter, all of three years old, ran around in excitement—closely followed by Kamala Bai, her nanny, who wore a Maharashtran *navvari* sari and had frizzy hair. Otima would never have been able to take care of the people of Bikaner, but for Kamala Bai who looked after the baby as if she were her own. She ran after the irrepressible toddler in the large grounds surrounding the Collector's Bungalow.

'Stop! That looks like a snake near that tree!' she exclaimed as she quickly scooped the child up in her arms and took her indoors, determined never to let her out of her sight.

Otima's office was sparse, but replete with the classic trappings of the office of a District Collector dating back to the times of the British Empire: inkpot, calligraphy pens, leather pads, blotting paper, and maps hanging on the walls. This was enough for her. She had simple tastes and did not need an ostentatious workplace. During her first week in the Collectorate, Otima realized how uncomfortable her staff was at having a woman as the Collector. After heated discussions, they had decided amongst themselves to address their new Collector as 'Collector Sa'ab' or just 'Sa'ab'.

It did not help that the collectorate had an all-male staff. Otima attracted additional attention due to the saris she wore in earthy hues—browns, beiges, bottle greens—not the classic bright Rajasthani colours, and certainly not the colours a married woman was supposed to wear in north India. She wore no glass bangles, no toe rings and no *mangal sutra* either. In fact, there was nothing to indicate her marital status—not even the red sindoor Bengali women applied in the parting of their hair. And, when she could, Otima wore high-heeled sandals, not the flat chappals all women in Rajasthan did.

Otima had always been a woman of firsts. One of India's first female IAS officers, her academic achievements are the stuff of legends at Allahabad University. So, being the only woman in the collectorate did not really bother her.

She found the culture of excessive—nay feudal—politeness in the spoken Hindi-Rajasthani rather disconcerting. But what truly bothered her was that no woman came to see her from the public. Even those who came for documents, or to lodge complaints, came with their families, their faces hidden behind a full ghoonghat—and never uttered a word!

She started a new tradition of leaving her office door open, ensuring that neither her personal secretary nor the office peon could act as gatekeepers and decide who could or could not meet her. Chairs were placed against the wall facing her, as well as in the veranda outside, for supplicants to sit while they waited for their turn. At that time, it was a major move towards transparency. Those waiting could vouch for her honour and objectivity. She heard everybody, regardless of a person's caste, class, religion, or political connections. A clear message went out that the new Collector, besides being efficient and fair, was accessible to one and all.

A fortnight after she joined as Collector, Bikaner. Otima noticed that groups of women clad in bright *lehenga-odhnis* came to her office almost every day. They would sit under the rickety fan and watch her quietly from behind their ghoonghats, as she went on with her work. After drinking cool water from the burnt-clay *matka*, they would leave without saying a word.

This continued for a few days. She had no idea as to what they wanted, or whether it was the same women that came in each day, for their faces were hidden behind their ghoonghats. One day, as a group of brightly dressed women drank water and rose to leave, Otima stopped them. She sent the men in the room outside, and shut the door to her office.

'Come, sit on these chairs.' Otima pointed to the chairs opposite her desk.

As the women sat down hesitantly at the edge of the seats, she asked the peon to bring more water for them.

'Now, tell me, where are you from? What do you want?'

There was total silence for a while, and then a soft voice from behind a red veil spoke for the entire group.

'Collector *Sa*, we are from Ambasar. We walked down from our village to see you.'

'Oh. But you came yesterday too, right?'

There was a tinkle of bangles and a giggle ran through the group. 'No, no—that wasn't us,' came the response.

'Those were women from Asera—a different village. They told us about you.'

'Okay. So, tell me, what can I do for you? But first you must lift your ghoonghats.'

There was an audible gasp of disbelief.

'How can I tell who you are unless I see you? From Asera or Ambasar?'

The peon walked into the room and put the glasses of water on the desk. Otima waited for him to leave, and then said something that sounded revolutionary to them. 'How do I know who you are behind your veil? And why do you wear such a long ghoonghat? Look, I am a wife and a mother like you. I am married into a Rajasthani family like yours. And, like you, I too place my pallav over my head, as is the tradition, to show respect to my in-laws, but I don't hide my face behind a veil. I know it must be claustrophobic for you, and that you can scarcely breathe in this heat. Take off the ghoonghat; don't stay cloistered behind it.'

Another gasp was heard from the back of the room, but Otima went on. 'Covering your head shows respect. A ghoonghat down to your waist seems to say, "I am scared of you; I am scared of showing my face to you." How can the strong and courageous women of Rajasthan be scared? You should fear none—no one at all!'

There was total silence as she spoke. No one took even a sip of water.

'And why should you be scared of me? I am here to help you. I may be the Collector of Bikaner, but I am a woman first. Come, remove your ghoonghat and talk to me without fear.'

And then the unbelievable occurred. An older woman—who looked about fifty—lifted her ghoonghat and smiled. The others followed suit. They were still a little tongue-tied, so Otima said, 'Now that I know who you are, tell me the problem. At least there will be no confusion. If the water in the village pond in Ambasar needs attention, the men won't go around cleaning the one in Asera!'

They all laughed and Otima was touched by the answer she received. 'We have no problem. We haven't come to you with any complaints,' said a young lady.

'We heard there was a woman Collector *Sa* in Bikaner, and came only to see her for ourselves.'

'I feel so proud to see you sitting on this chair—we all do,' said the older woman who had lifted her veil first.

Otima was pleasantly surprised. A group of women had left their important chores in the village, and walked for miles in the sun over the hot sand, only to see with their own eyes a woman who had become the Collector of their district—all exulting internally in another step forward for women.

After that, several women would come with their families, clad in lehnga odhni with a long ghoonghat. They would ask to see her alone to discuss their problems, and remove their veils in her presence, though behind closed doors. It was 1965—a good beginning. For the first time, women in the district of Bikaner could actually talk to the Collector.

There was nothing Otima enjoyed more than being out in the field, where she could meet people. This was essential, for Otima had landed in the district during a vicious drought. In the next three years, she realized that drought was a way of life. It occurred every year, without fail. She memorized the 'Famine Code'—chapter and verse. The city girl was out and about, overseeing drought relief work and trying to understand the problems of the citizens in remote villages. The heady feeling that her actions were changing people's lives drove her harder.

In this almost foreign culture, what would Otima have done without Surja Ramji, her driver? He was on the brink of retirement. He had been raised in the usual Rajasthani tradition of loyalty, and polite but brutal honesty. She spent a great deal of time on the road, as she toured the district constantly and held camp offices. Surja Ramji became her assistant and guide. He had a brilliant memory, possessed strong knowledge of the politics of the area, and understood the pulse of the people. He steered her gently along the rigid dos and don'ts of Rajasthani culture. She learnt to curb her desire to talk with the villagers rather than listen to the interlocutors.

Having been integrated with the Union of India in 1949, Bikaner in the 1960s was still in the process of learning to be a district and not a kingdom. Many of the processes, and much of the culture, of the old Bikaner state still existed. Local politics was evolving. Not everyone was happy with the intrepid young female Collector, who was constantly out in the villages. Local politicians often put roadblocks in her way. Several members of her own staff were unhappy because she did not accept the reports from them unquestioningly, believing in their ostensible truth and objectivity. Instead, she would go to the field herself on random inspections.

If there was one thing Otima detested, it was bullying and blackmail. Even the slightest suspicion that her hand was being forced riled her to the point where she had to turn to her inner voice to calm herself. She had to control her fiery side and talk to some local leaders who, she felt, posed some kind of threat to the district administration. She was adept at the 'who-will-blink-first' game.

After a few months, she became more familiar with the terrain, the culture, and the politics of Bikaner—and the people of Bikaner got used to her and her ways. In May, the news of increasing skirmishes along the international border in other states created a buzz. Otima wanted to see the Indo-Pak border along the north-western edge of Bikaner district. Surja Ramji drove her in a jeep through the desert to where the shifting sand dunes marked an ill-defined *de facto* international dividing line. Her Sub-Divisional Officer (SDO), Superintendant of Police (SP) and tehsildar, accompanied her. That evening, the sun had gone down and it had become dark as they left the desert to return to Bikaner town.

'Where are we headed, Surja Ramji?' Otima asked as she peered into the darkness.

'*Kuchh to dekha hua hai, sa'ab* [I have seen some of the area before, and am familiar with it],' Surja Ramji murmured as he looked up at the star-studded desert sky. '*Aur baaki taare dekhte dekhte pahunch jaayenge, sa'ab.* [As for the rest, we will reach there somehow, guided by the stars, sir.]'

Otima was rather wary of what seemed like her driver's overconfidence. Those were the days when traffic lights on highways were unheard of—leave alone on village roads and *kachcha* tracks across the sand dunes. She was pleasantly surprised when the mission ended successfully, without a single wrong turn under the starry sky. Surja Ramji himself was her North Star in more ways than one.

And then, without much warning, the Indo-Pak War broke out. The 1965 War was a culmination of brief encounters between Pakistan and India. The skirmishes had started along the border in other districts in April 1965—around the time that Otima made history in Rajasthan as the first woman Collector of Bikaner. Four months later, in September 1965, there was a full-scale military attack on West Pakistan. The seventeen-day war resulted in thousands of casualties on both sides.

The largest engagement of armoured vehicles took place along the Indo-Pak border in 1965, and was the biggest tank battle since World War II.

Right before the war broke out, an agitation by university students, whose leaders were aligned with different political parties, also rocked Bikaner. Their protest for more teachers, and seats in professional institutions, had turned violent and taken up much of Otima's time. Once the war broke out in September, the agitation became a thing of the past.

The Indian Army crossed the International Border on the Western front on 6 September 1965.

The hostilities in Rajasthan commenced officially two days later—on 8 September—when a Company of the 5 Maratha Light Infantry was sent to reinforce the Rajasthan Armed Constabulary, at the border post in Munabao—a strategic hamlet about 250 kilometres from Jodhpur. Bikaner district, along with the districts of Jodhpur, Jaisalmer, Barmer and Ganganagar, shared a border with West Pakistan.

'The war was the most memorable period of my career,' Otima reminisced years later in front of her children.

Most of the battles in Rajasthan were fought by opposing infantry and armoured units as well as by camel units in the Thar, with air cover as a backup. The 13th Battalion, which, inter alia, included the Bikaner Camel Corps, took part in the valiant action on the Rajasthan border. They foiled the Pakistani Army in Bikaner and Jaisalmer.

Pakistan made some gains, although initially the Pakistan Desert Force and the Hur militia were placed in a defensive role. The Hurs—followers of Pir Pagaro—were familiar with the terrain and possessed essential desert survival skills. They inflicted many casualties on the Indian forces as they entered from Sindh. Before September, they often indulged in clashes on camels to harass the Indians along the Line of Control (LoC). Come September, when the Indo-Pak War broke out, they attacked and captured several villages in Rajasthan. The District Magistrate of Bikaner became an important part of the action on the Indian side of the border.

By May, soon after Operation Desert Hawk was launched in the Rann of Kutch, Otima had started thinking of the possibilities of war. She was rather far-sighted. In August, after Operation Gibraltar, the district administration in Bikaner started planning for the war efforts in all earnest, under her directions. A Civil Protection Plan for Bikaner District, which provided a measure of civil defence, was organized, primarily on a voluntary basis with a small nucleus of paid staff.

A group of volunteers was identified and trained in various fields, including first aid, to assist them in the event of any emergency. Amongst other things, the volunteers also helped the community dig trenches and bunkers for protection during a possible air raid, throughout August. Community air raid shelters were dug for the poor.

'Aren't you overthinking?' her batchmate, the Collector of one of the neighbouring districts, had chuckled over a trunk call. 'I believe you have begun advanced planning. These skirmishes have been going on since April. How can you assume there will be a war?'

'I am assuming nothing—I only want to be prepared for all possibilities,' Otima had replied.

For a while, she pondered over the conversation. Was she being too cautious? And then she put her reservations behind her and went ahead with the plans. She started ensuring that food supplies, and supplies of medicines and essential drugs, did not run short.

Drinking water was a major issue in the drought-prone district, despite the presence of the Ganga Canal, completed in 1928. Otima and the Chief Engineer of the district, Mohan Asthana, visited the canal to see if it needed repair. They also inspected water works and other drinking-water facilities in the district. Public health engineers were sent out to ensure that all the stepwells and ponds in the villages across the district were well-maintained, and that the handpumps were in working condition.

Otima undertook several inspections of hospitals and health centres across the districts along with Dr Bhatnagar, the Chief Medical Officer (CMO), to ensure preparedness. August onwards, no government doctor or health worker was allowed leave. Leave sanctioned earlier by the CMO was cancelled. All medical personnel were directed to remain in their headquarters.

Several executive orders were issued in view of the impending war. A few orders would not have stood up in a court of law under normal circumstances. One executive order Otima passed in August caused a great deal of heartburn, but she considered it important. The order stated that any officer could be assigned any duty by the Collector, in public interest, until the war was over. Refusal to perform the work so assigned would tantamount to dereliction of duty, and would invite disciplinary proceedings. Every government officer and official in the district of Bikaner—across different organizations, including the engineering departments—was asked to remain within the district.

Otima knew that she had exercised powers she did not possess. Yet, it was essential given the circumstances. She forwarded a copy of the order to their respective head offices in Jaipur—and then went ahead to develop a roster for wartime duties for them.

By the end of August, war seemed imminent. As the District Magistrate, it was Otima's responsibility to liaise with the army personnel. She was in constant touch with her counterparts in the Indian Army and the Border Security Force (BSF). Staying in touch with Delhi was a difficult proposition. Even a 'lightning call' to Delhi sometimes took twenty-four hours. Communication channels with the state headquarters were few and far between.

As the war loomed large, Otima issued an executive order for a night vigil by the community leaders. In view of her responsibilities as the head of the district, it was necessary to develop a system to protect the public, the vital services, and the facilities in her territory. She put together a system that immediately set off a siren on receipt of information about an impending air raid, and another to announce the end of danger. As the war broke out, Otima imposed a night curfew. The community was made aware of the Standard Operating Procedures (SOPs) of a blackout, through loudspeakers, during the day.

Stocks of food grains had been replenished by the time the war broke out, as Otima had made concerted efforts in August to ensure sufficient food stock. Cereals and cooking oil were rationed, as was kerosene—the main fuel for cooking. She had also issued an order to stop fodder from being transferred out of the district to maintain a reserve for the cattle. A rationing system for petrol and diesel was also put in place for private vehicles.

One incident that still rankles Otima occurred on the fifteenth day of the seventeen-day war. Even as she did what she did, Otima knew it was not right. Her actions went against the values ingrained in her. Yet, even now, fifty-five years later, she feels no remorse. When she looks back, she believes she would have taken the same decisions under similar circumstances.

Despite the rationing, food stocks declined rapidly in the Food and Civil Supplies godowns. A fortnight into the war, the stocks of the district were almost over. No one knew how long the battle would continue. Several Rajasthani villages had already been taken over by Pakistan's Desert Force with the support of the Hurs.

Otima checked the depleted stocks, and was concerned that the people of Bikaner might starve if the food stocks were not replenished. The Sub-Divisional Magistrate (SDM) informed her that a godown of the recently established Food Corporation of India (FCI) was full of wheat and bajra (millet). Otima issued an executive order to requisition the foodgrains stocked with the FCI, in public interest. She was told that the order could not be executed as the godown was locked and the local manager had fled from the district along with the keys. Otima had sent a copy of the requisitioning order to the FCI head office, based in Madras those days, but even a lightning call to that city was not possible. She pondered for a while, and looked up as a fighter plane flew overhead—thankfully, Indian.

Then she did something she would never have done, but for the fact that the only other option was to let the people of Bikaner starve. After all, a war *was* on.

'Go break the lock.'

'Madam?' The SDM was flabbergasted.

Otima saw the SDM look at her in astonishment. He was a young boy, who had barely put in three years of service. She knew she should explain herself.

'Look, I know under normal circumstances we would wait for the manager to return and personally hand over the stock we have requisitioned, to us. But these are not normal times. The man is not coming back before the war is over. And God only knows how long it will go on . . . Who knows if we will come out alive . . .?' she said, as she heard the shelling in the distance. 'I can't let the people of Bikaner die of hunger when a godown full of foodgrains I have already requisitioned, exists within the district, merely because an irresponsible man has chosen to abandon his duty.'

'True, Collector Sa'ab! We have already issued the requisitioning order. The treasury will pay for it from the exchequer once the war is over,' said a Revenue Officer, and the tehsildar.

'Yes, this is wartime! And a war needs contingency plans.' The SDM nodded heartily in agreement.

She said to the SDM, 'Go then. But, even during a war, we must ensure that the process is duly followed. You and the tehsildar should take three more officers with you. Please count every gunny sack, weigh it in your presence, and maintain an account. Mark the foodgrains on your stock register. Ensure all five of you sign every page of the register. Then place a new double lock on the door. Give one key to the tehsildar and keep one yourself . . . and start distributing the rations from this afternoon.'

'Hukum.'

Otima sighed with relief. With the additional food stock, the situation would be comfortable for another fortnight. She looked westwards. Already two weeks had passed and, hearing more shells in the distance, she wondered when the fighting would end.

Two days later, on 22 September, Otima received a frantic call from home. Her daughter's finger had been caught in the door and she was screaming with pain. She rushed home to find that the finger had been attended to, and that the toddler had cried herself to sleep. As she bent down over her three-year-old, she smelt her soft hair and tried to remember when she had last played with the little one, or when she would be able to in the future. She kissed her daughter's cheek, thinking about how her life would turn out—with no inkling that she and this little girl would become the first mother-daughter pair in the IAS—when the siren indicating an impending air raid went off.

Otima picked her daughter up in her arms gently, and started walking towards the trench. Anil, her husband, reminded her that it was the seventeenth day of the war. It was the first time she was entering the trench with her family.

Anil had managed everything on the home front. He had supervised the digging of multiple trenches in the premises of the Collector's house—meant to be air raid shelters for the Bordia family during an air attack—but usually meant for Anil, his little daughter, and the staff in the Collector's Bungalow. Otima was never there, because she was out patrolling the area through the night with the Superintendent of Police (SP) and sometimes with her BSF and army counterparts. How could she not be where the action was?

The District Magistrate had patrolled Bikaner town, and a major part of the district, every night for the last seventeen days. Otima had not slept a wink. She barely ate, and saw her family only when she came home early in the morning every day for a short break and some breakfast. She and the

SP had to ensure a strict vigil. The maintenance of curfew, as well as the blackouts, to pre-empt an air raid were crucial. Keeping Bikaner and the other towns and villages calm was an important role of the district administration. It had been imperative to instil confidence, and a sense of security, amongst the community.

As the siren sounded on the evening of 22 September, Otima entered the air raid shelter with her sleeping three-year-old in her arms. Seventeen days after the war had begun, she looked around at the secure haven her husband had got built meticulously for their safety. Putting the baby in her lap, she stretched her tired limbs, smiled, and yawned at the same time.

'This is fancy. You've done a great job; it's almost like *Alice in Wonderland's* little—' She was fast asleep before she could complete her sentence.

Anil smiled and took their daughter from her arms. He laid a cushion under his wife's tired head, and stretched her legs. He let the overworked Collector of Bikaner sleep through the air raid. She slept like a baby even after a siren signalled that the raid was over and it was safe to leave the bunkers and trenches.

Anil put their daughter on the bed in the house gently. Otima slept on in the trench. She slept through the night—and almost half of the next morning—for the first time since the war had broken out.

On the morning of 23 September, when the hostility between the two countries ended after a ceasefire mandated by the United Nations was declared, it was Anil who received the message—while the Collector of Bikaner slept in the trench.

Coda

Otima's tenure as the Collector of Bikaner was like being on a three-year-long high. Even today, she says it was the most exciting time of her life—and not just her career. She left Bikaner, fulfilled and happy.

Soon, it was time to move to a slower pace. Otima and her husband received fellowships to go to Canada for training. It was time for the couple to spend more hours together and to be exposed to a world outside their own.

She went on to become the Finance Secretary of Rajasthan. She also did two stints in the central government. The first was at the Director and Joint Secretary-level in the Ministry of Power. The second was as Additional Secretary, and later, as a Secretary. She served in the Prime Minister's Office and in the Ministries of Finance, Industries, and Chemicals and Fertilizers.

She left the government to serve as a member of the Union Public Service Commission, where she worked until she was sixty-five. Her retirement years have been spent reading, travelling, taking care of her mother, spending time with her grandchildren, and reflecting on life.

II

Saving Lives

An unknown unseen innocuous form
an invisible virus of despair and doom . . .

The last victim of wild polio in India was a girl child called Rukhsar Khatoon from Howrah.

'She's suffering because of me! Why did I not get my Rukhsar vaccinated? We gave her brother those two drops of vaccine, but we did not give them to her,' her father, Abdul Shah, lamented.

Since 1988, the polio virus had caused havoc in the lives of millions of children. It had led to acute flaccid paralysis in their limbs. The debilitation, for which there was no cure, lasted all their lives. For more than two decades, India had been fighting against polio valiantly. The end of this long battle was nowhere in sight even at the turn of the century. There was growing fatigue, despair and hopelessness.

Then, all of a sudden, a turnaround happened a little after Anuradha Gupta joined the Health Ministry in the

Government of India. She led a team that helped the country achieve a hitherto elusive goal. India reported its last case of wild polio on 13 January 2011. The country has been free of polio ever since.

'Thank God the obdurate polio virus has now been relegated to history in India!' Anuradha mused.

The Deputy CEO of Global Alliance for Vaccines and Immunization (GAVI) recalled her battle against polio, as she watched the sunset on the shores of Lake Genève on her way back from office in Geneva. GAVI, like the rest of the world, was combating a new virus in 2020–2021 that needed to be vanquished globally. Anuradha looked at the setting sun, and began to reminisce about her successful battle against the disease in India a few years earlier.

Rukhsar's father, Abdul Shah, had been devastated when his daughter fell victim to the polio virus. He could not undo the harm caused to his own child, but was determined to help prevent others from making the mistakes he had made. Full of remorse, he became a strong 'polio vaccine advocate'. He would carry Rukhsar on his shoulders, walk door-to-door, with tears in his eyes, urge reluctant parents to vaccinate their children, for 'seeing is believing', he would often say. Rukhsar, with her paralyzed legs, was a living symbol of his negligence and shame.

'Only two drops! Two drops are your way of telling your child you care. And, if you are negligent—like I was with *my* Rukhsar—see what can happen!' he would implore with moist, pleading eyes.

Awareness generation was a major factor in helping eradicate polio. A father's appeal played an important role in saving lives by reaching the reluctant parents of many 'children who had been missed or ignored'.

'Rukhsar's father's entreaty was probably more effective than even that of the megastar, Amitabh Bachan. Our polio brand ambassador was brilliant, but Rukhsar and her father made a more forceful and compelling case,' Anuradha thought.

She smiled to herself as she recalled her uphill journey in her battle against polio almost a decade ago. As the sun went down, she sighed and climbed into her car to drive home to her quaint cottage in Tannay, a small suburb on the outskirts of Geneva.

'Well that was India and the polio virus. And now it's the whole world up against the coronavirus . . . I guess viruses have a strange connection with my life. What a horrific pandemic it has caused! The world just has to find a solution soon—and GAVI must play its part in that solution.' Anuradha looked pensively over the lake. She noticed that the sun had almost set behind the Swiss Alps overlooking the water. The sky was splashed with beautiful shades of amber and orange. She was reminded of another exotic sunset over a different lake surrounded by the Shivalik Hills in Chandigarh . . . for that was where her voyage had begun.

One day, around sunset, Anuradha was walking around Sukhna Lake with Praveen, her husband and batchmate, in the Indian Administrative Service, when her mobile phone rang. It was an unexpected call from the Union Health Secretary. He asked her whether she would be willing to join the Ministry of Health and Family Welfare, Government of India. She would replace the Joint Secretary, National Rural Health Mission (NRHM), who had completed his tenure.

Anuradha was torn between saying yes and no. As the Health Secretary, Haryana, she had introduced several reforms. This was her opportunity to work on a larger canvas and the NRHM was a dream job! However, moving to GoI meant separation from her husband. Life in Chandigarh was peaceful, and Praveen was unwilling to throw himself into the crazy din and pollution of Delhi.

The couple continued their walk, considering the pros and cons of the sudden and unexpected offer. Near the end of the jogging track, they met a colleague who had just finished his run. He waved and then joined them. He was incredulous that Anuradha was taking time to reflect on whether or not to take up the offer, as he had been encouraging her to consider deputation with the Centre seriously for some time now.

'What! How can you even consider spurning such an attractive opportunity? Go, Anuradha!'

'I guess I am lucky to be asked to work at the national level in the Health Ministry. It is a sector that has been my most rewarding professional experience in Haryana,' Anuradha replied, tempted to go.

'Not merely lucky, Anu. The call is a result of your commitment and hard work. Look at the change you have driven in Haryana as the Health Secretary. In a province lagging behind on all public-health indices, you have successfully demonstrated that progress is possible.'

'Actually, it is truly ironic that my posting as the Health Secretary in Haryana has become an all-consuming passion, despite the fact that it appears rather lacklustre to many of our colleagues within the cadre.' Anuradha smiled.

'I also think you should consider going to Delhi seriously, Anu. How many people get their dream job offered to them on a platter over the phone?' said Parveen, not wanting to hold his wife back.

Government-hospital administrators in Haryana had a laissez-faire attitude. The hospitals suffered from a shortage of doctors, drugs and diagnostics. There was no link between patient load and budget allocation by the government. Often a hospital with a high caseload ended up being allotted the same budget and number of staff members as one with a lower footfall.

The state's health policy needed to be revised with the changing times. Anuradha toured the region extensively, and found that the distribution of the workforce in the health department was highly skewed across the state. The rural centres were understaffed and lacked doctors and health personnel. In sharp contrast, the urban ones were both coveted and overstaffed—partly due to loopholes in the policy, but more due to lack of will. Most of the doctors in the overstaffed, and yet under-performing urban facilities, were connected to powerful politicians and bureaucrats. She was surprised to see that in a well-equipped district hospital with 200 beds, the occupancy was a mere 28 per cent: This, despite the fact that there was a massive slum population surrounding it with no access to healthcare.

Patients were turned away from government hospitals even for routine services, and redirected to private nursing homes that had sprouted within a five-kilometre radius. Many government medical officers had their own roaring private practice. They often coerced their patients to pay the fees for services rendered privately outside the government premises. Some CMOs turned a blind eye to the collusion between such malpractitioners.

The understaffed rural centres deprived the rural population of the access to good healthcare. The staff was often absent and, sometimes, the centres were found locked up during surprise inspections!

Anuradha acted swiftly and decisively to curb these malpractices.

'Gosh, she seems to be everywhere! This Health Secretary means business'— was the common opinion.

Unavailability of medicines in the government facilities was a matter of concern. Though more than Rs 10,00,00,000 were spent annually to buy medicines for patients in the government hospitals, nobody knew how those medicines were used or distributed. Many of them rotted in the hospital stores, some were resold to chemists and some reserved for the VIPs. Patients were informed that the drugs were out of stock, and they were given prescriptions to buy them from other chemists and pharmacies.

An association of chemists once visited Anuradha and told her something that horrified her. They said, 'Madam, our business is ruined. Doctors in the local government hospital prescribe unknown brands stocked only by a few chemists—those that provide kickbacks.'

She discovered a booming nexus between some doctors, chemists and pharmaceutical companies. Some doctors prescribed what were known locally as 'propaganda drugs', which essentially meant substandard drugs from smaller unknown firms, but priced even higher than the well-established brands. Doctors, pharmaceutical companies and chemists who were part of the unholy nexus flourished, while the patients suffered because of the low efficacy of the propaganda drugs bought at inflated prices.

Anuradha knew the malaise ran deep. Some very powerful people had vested interests in the racket, but she was unfazed. She put an array of reforms in motion. For the first time there was a clear, well publicized policy, which entitled every patient to free essential drugs.

'Why everybody? Why not only those below the poverty line, the BPL?' —was a question often asked.

Anuradha would smile and say, 'Well, the BPL criterion has existed forever for most government schemes, but it has flaws. Let us keep things simple and transparent. In any case, mostly families who cannot afford out-of-pocket-expenses are the ones who visit the government facilities. The rich go to private hospitals.'

Transparent systems were put in place for bulk procurement and efficient distribution. High volumes drove the competition and prices dropped. The budget was enough to guarantee free essential medicines to everyone visiting the government health facilities. Public awareness increased dramatically.

'And now even villagers dare to ask me strange questions,' the head of a primary health centre lamented.

His colleague agreed. 'The other day a man wanted to know why I was asking him to buy an anti-rabies injection from the chemist, when my quota for the month pasted on the wall said I still had twelve vials in the store.'

'I had to placate an angry crowd outside my health centre, as we ran out of Paracetamol. The local cable-network unit mocked my poor management. And the Deputy Commissioner called for an explanation,' a doctor complained.

'I am losing the extra money I had become so used to,' said a paramedic.

'We have to take this to the highest levels . . .'

Around this time, Anuradha decided it was time to meet the Chief Minister (CM) of Haryana. She walked into the CM's camp office at his official residence and asked to see him. She was called in immediately. She explained at length the problems that beset the state's health department, and how she was making policy interventions to improve the systems and processes.

'Medicines and healthcare are matters of life and death, sir,' she said. 'No one should be allowed to play with people's lives—it is immoral.'

The CM listened to her intently and was unequivocal in his praise. 'You have my full support. Please keep up the good work.'

Anuradha later heard that the CM had snubbed a delegation of people who had met him to seek her transfer, amongst other things.

'The health of my people is important. Do not expect me to back immoral interests,' he had said to the delegation firmly.

After that, there was no looking back for Anuradha. She received a nod of approval from the CM even for matters deemed radical—such as a rolling system for the doctors' recruitment. The health workforce was distributed rationally. Performance-based incentives were provided for difficult areas. User fees were abolished for several essential services.

The infrastructure in government hospitals and peripheral facilities were upgraded. Private practice by government doctors was curbed with a heavy hand. Absenteeism in the field was checked, performance was closely monitored and run through a system of rewards and penalties. Pregnant women were guaranteed no-expense deliveries in the government facilities. They could dial an emergency helpline on 102 for a free ambulance. Children began to be screened for the early detection of diseases.

It was gratifying to see the quick and measurable impact brought about by the reforms. The daily dashboard kept climbing with each intervention: number of outpatients, bed occupancy, surgeries performed, essential drugs distributed, children screened, institutional births, free transport utilization and availability of the health workforce. Three new government medical colleges and a satellite campus of the All India Institute of Medical Sciences, in the state, were unprecedented strides in tertiary healthcare. Haryana began to improve its coverage and quality of primary healthcare too. Maternal and child mortality came down. Out-of-pocket expenses on health matters declined. The small but strategic policy interventions made a huge difference through strengthened systems and streamlined processes. The focus on healthcare went a long way in improving the health indices of the state across the spectrum.

'What's happening in Haryana? They are doing some amazing things!'—was a common discussion at national-level meetings.

The Union Health Secretary often said, 'There seems to be a spate of good practices in Haryana that can be emulated by other states and replicated across the country.'

The phone call from the Health Secretary on that fortunate evening seemed to open a floodgate of opportunities for Anuradha on a larger canvas. Praveen had always provided wings to his wife's dreams. He encouraged her to apply formally for a central deputation, and the tenacious Union Secretary ensured she joined the Health Ministry. However, she was not given the charge of NRHM that she had so looked forward to. Instead, she was assigned Reproductive and Child Health (RCH). Soon she understood why.

India had the largest share of global maternal and child deaths. At a time when progress on Millennium Development Goals (MDGs) was an international priority, the challenge needed to be addressed expeditiously. UN Secretary General, Ban Ki-moon, had launched an 'Every Woman Every Child' strategy. The day Anuradha joined the ministry, in 2010, the Secretary flew out to New York to make a statement on behalf of India, but was concerned at the lack of a credible national strategy or plan, and wanted Anuradha to help work on it.

India was also amongst the last four countries of the world with the 'ongoing transmission of the wild polio virus'. Nigeria, Pakistan and Afghanistan were the only other countries struggling with it in a similar manner. Together, the three accounted for half of the global polio cases, while India contributed to the remaining half.

Percentages, when translated into actual numbers of polio victims in India, were alarming. Internationally, concerns about the country's ability to eradicate the scourge were mounting. India was seen as a reservoir of the polio virus.

The Global Polio Eradication Initiative (GPEI) was the largest public health programme in history. This flagship

World Health Organization (WHO) programme was
launched in 1988. Technical leadership was provided by the
international organizations such as WHO, the United Nations
Children's Fund (UNICEF), and the Centers for Disease
Control and Prevention (CDC). Rotary International also
embraced polio eradication as their top priority, and many
voluntary organizations joined in to support the endeavour
globally. An array of development partners and private
foundations contributed large sums of money. Political will
was mobilized at the highest levels in all countries across the
globe. The stakes were very high. They envisioned that after
smallpox, polio would be the second disease to be wiped off
the face of the earth.

Vaccination was the prime method of eradication. The
Global Polio Eradication Initiative was intended to be a time-
bound effort, with the aim of completing the job in a couple
of years. Despite the passage of more than twenty years of
ongoing polio vaccination campaigns across the world, the
reality was that, in 2010, the virus was yet to be vanquished.
Billions of dollars had been invested and the future still
looked pretty uncertain. There was a real risk of backsliding.

India, which contributed to half of the world's polio
burden, had to make a concerted bid to get rid of a disease
that had crippled millions of Indian children for life. Against
this backdrop, Anuradha set out on a journey to help make
India polio free.

A fortnight after joining service as Joint Secretary, Health,
GoI, she attended a global polio review meeting. Countries,
much poorer than India, had succeeded in ridding themselves
of the wild polio virus much earlier. She was embarrassed

when India was called out by the rest of the world for a dismal performance. Less developed countries were being hailed for their impressive progress. The forum was optimistic that Nigeria would soon reach the zero-case level.

The global discontent at India's lack of progress was palpable. The country was holding back the global march towards a polio-free world. Despite continuous efforts for nearly twenty years, the end was nowhere in sight even in 2010. Everyone was watching India closely as the one nation that needed to play a prime role in making the global dream come true.

'What needs to change?' Anuradha pondered over the issue.

Almost fifteen long years earlier, on 9 December 1995, India had embarked upon a strategy reliant on mass polio immunization campaigns called the 'Pulse Polio' rounds. Every year, two rounds were held, four to six weeks apart, usually in January and February. It was a mammoth undertaking, and the whole nation was involved in a bid to triumph over the disease as soon as possible. The aim was to provide oral polio drops to every child under the age of five.

Eradicating polio was an important national priority and everybody strived to contribute. India's polio awareness and eradication programme had many vital components. Celebrities with mass appeal passionately espoused the cause. A district task force under the Collector's leadership coordinated each polio campaign. Railways, Defence, Civil Aviation, Surface Transport, Urban Development and all other major ministries were involved. Besides the commitment of the government and civil society, unprecedented global solidarity brought together a large and diverse set of stakeholders who provided generous funds to support the polio vaccination campaigns. Every national Pulse Polio campaign was launched by the President of India—a tradition that had not been violated even once since 1995.

During a national Pulse Polio round, more than 20,00,000 frontline health workers, Aanganwadi workers, and volunteers, fanned out to knock at the doors of crores of households. They provided polio drops to nearly 17,00,00,000 children under the age of five. Thousands of supervisors were out in the field to oversee this large-scale operation. Independent monitors provided additional assurance. The fact that the programme was able to sustain its momentum for a decade and a half was nothing less than a miracle.

Children across the nation, including those travelling on trains, buses, airplanes, boats, and those living on mountain tops or in slums, drain pipes, around brick kilns, on construction sites, refuse dumps; or in river basins, or nomad settlements were to be reached with *do boond zindagi ke'* or 'two drops of life'.

The Pulse Polio strategy had succeeded in interrupting the transmission of the polio virus in most parts of the country by 1999. However, in several areas, it still persisted, particularly in western Uttar Pradesh, central Bihar, and pockets of Jharkhand and West Bengal. The megacities of Delhi, Mumbai and Kolkata became hotbeds of the virus because of incessant migration.

Polio is a deadly disease and can spread even if one child is left uncovered. Subnational Pulse Polio rounds were hence introduced in 1999 and carried out with regular frequency.

Multiple rounds of subnational Pulse Polio were conducted up to eight times a year, over and above the two national campaigns in January-February. Emergency mop ups were also done as and when polio struck. A child belonging to an endemic area, where polio persisted, might possibly have received a polio vaccine as many as twelve times in a year. Over the years, the returns from these rounds diminished.

The importance that the government attached to the polio campaigns was evident from the fact that the budget for them was nearly two-and-a-half times more than that of the Universal Immunization Programme—for equitable access to a range of vaccines against other diseases besides polio, including BCG (Bacille Calmette-Guerin), DTP (diphtheria, tetanus, pertussis), Hepatitis B and measles for children; and tetanus for pregnant women. The collateral damage of these inequities in the allocation of funds was that while polio vaccination was able to achieve a high coverage because of the campaigns, the full immunization programme hovered around 62 per cent only—as against the 90 per cent coverage for polio alone. Many parents were unaware of the other vaccines equally important for the protection of their children.

Incessant campaigns had helped bring down the number of annual polio cases. Yet, eradication was nowhere in sight. The GoI largely funded India's polio programme, but was reliant on the WHO's National Polio Surveillance Project (NPSP), to guide and manage the programme. The India Expert Advisory Group (IEAG) comprised a galaxy of global and national experts, including experts from WHO headquarters and the Centers for Disease Control and

Prevention (CDC). The group met twice every year to review the programme and to recommend the number and scope of polio-specific campaigns.

Prior to Anuradha's arrival in 2010, the IEAG meetings involved lengthy reviews and often ended up being 'blame games'. Health Secretaries from the endemic states that suffered continuous transmission of the wild polio virus, such as Uttar Pradesh and Bihar, came under intense scrutiny, as did the technical agencies such as WHO and UNICEF. The focus was more on defending oneself against criticism. The elephant in the room was completely ignored.

The last reservoirs of the lurking virus were proving to be intractable. There was despair all around. India bore the brunt of the one-size-fits-all approach. The global strategy was entirely predicated on repetitive campaigns. Anuradha was convinced that India had to tailor its own country-specific solutions to ensure 100 per cent vaccination coverage to eradicate the virus once and for all.

To arrive at an efficacious strategy, it was imperative to understand why success had been elusive so far. Multiple reasons, inherent in the geography, climate, demography, socio-economic factors, and the religious and cultural norms, prevailed in India. With 27,00,00,00 new births in the country, the size of the annual cohort that needed to be vaccinated every year on an ongoing basis was astoundingly large. The reach of basic health services, including routine vaccines, was low. There were formidable challenges in reaching children in remote and inaccessible geographies. Poverty, open defecation, contaminated food and water, worm infestations, poor hygiene and malnutrition, compounded the issue. Added to this was the challenge of the burgeoning migrant population in urban and peri-urban settlements and slums. Given the large-scale mobility within the country, the follow-up of families and children was extremely difficult. The task was daunting, but not impossible.

'Why is the programme stuck at 90 per cent coverage even after fifteen years of frequent well-budgeted, campaigns?' Anuradha wondered, wanting to get to the bottom of the problem.

She asked for the statistics of the last fifteen years to understand the trouble. As she sought the data from her team, she explained the vital importance of gathering, analyzing and interpreting data to pinpoint a problem—and then to seek solutions.

'Understanding data is the first important step.'

'Yes, Ma'am,' said Dr Ajay Khera, a public health enthusiast, as he stared at her, clueless about where the conversation was headed.

'Look at the generous budget for the polio campaigns. Compare it with the routine immunization budget. Notice the additional remuneration we have been providing to every health worker, supervisor and monitor, for each Pulse Polio round. It's so attractive . . .'

'Ma'am, the incentive has indeed been large, and increasing on the premise that the higher the incentive, the more sincerely the health workforce will perform,' said Dr Haider, who was in charge of the immunization programme.

'Well, it doesn't seem to have worked so far. I wonder if it is now time to re-examine that premise. A campaign should be a time-bound, focused attack on the problem—

with a clearly defined end. We have been in a campaign mode to eradicate polio for nearly fifteen years now. The rest of the world, except for three other nations, has moved on successfully.' She paused as she looked at the figures before her again. 'How can we allow our children to suffer as we meander forever? Aren't we also encouraging the desire to have Pulse Polio campaigns until eternity—with no end in sight?'

'I see, Ma'am. You mean it suits everyone to have perpetual polio campaigns?'

'Maybe. I don't know . . . All I know is that more Pulse Polio rounds mean more money. And despite the money poured into the campaigns over the last fifteen years, we continue to be in campaign mode and the end continues to be elusive. The polio campaigns definitely have a higher budget than the Universal Immunization Programme (UIP) through which we deliver polio and other vaccines without campaigns.'

Dr Khera nodded in agreement as he saw the funding pattern.

'Apparently, the circle of beneficiaries from our campaigns is much larger; it includes many more than our own health workers. Programme managers perhaps find it easy to recycle banners and publicity materials to reach the same children over and over again, year after year. Monitors get a handsome honorarium. Everyone finds it easy to pocket money that flows freely. We have spent nearly Rs 10,00,00,00,00,00 in the last fifteen years and yet not eradicated the wretched disease! Our children continue to suffer. We are obviously doing something wrong.'

'Gosh. Ma'am, we never quite saw it from that perspective.'

'I believe we need to relook at our strategy and undertake several activities critical to locating children, who were left out in each successive vaccination round. Rather than spreading our efforts thinly, let us shift our focus from only measuring the number of children covered to tracking, and shining a light upon the number of "missing children".'

On joining office as Joint Secretary, RCH, Anuradha learnt that the ministry had virtually outsourced the leadership and running of India's polio eradication initiative to WHO's National Polio Surveillance Project (the NPSP), partly due to the heavy portfolio of the Joint Secretary (JS), RCH. The WHO Project had the best talent of 300 medical officers from all the states, and offered much higher salaries than what they received in the government.

The NPSP owned the data, funded surveillance, conducted analytics and designed the technical strategies. Surveillance officers of the NPSP were present in all the states to make sure that the Pulse Polio rounds followed the standard drill, including the launch by the Governor of the state. They compiled all the reports, relayed them at the global level, and represented India at the Polio International Monitoring Board—a board set up to review countries' progress critically. Over the years, the polio eradication campaign had been spearheaded almost entirely by the NPSP—and the Ministry of Health had taken a back seat.

Anuradha decided to change the existing dynamics and take the responsibility head on. She took charge resolutely, and became involved with planning, monitoring, and following up on every single polio round. The future of the children was at stake. To understand the ground conditions, a series of brainstorming sessions were held. Field functionaries were invited and asked to share their experiences with the officers in the ministry, functionaries from the NPSP and from the state governments.

'Eradication of polio from the soil of India is our shared dream . . . and the absolute responsibility of the Government of India in partnership with the states. We can't shirk our responsibility and leave it only to the NPSP or any other partner agency. They are here to support our efforts but, please, from now on, let us all take charge. Lack of success is no longer an option,' Anuradha paused as she looked at the animated faces of all the experienced people around the table. 'We are determined to succeed—and soon. Let us start identifying the gaps. Unless we see what we have not been doing right for the last decade and a half, we will continue to make the same mistakes.'

'Ma'am, I am so happy we are having this discussion. Many parents I have met are becoming increasingly resistant to their children receiving countless vaccine doses,' said a field functionary.

'Some communities are suspicious about why the government is focusing on polio.'

'Yes, Ma'am, there is growing resentment over the lack of attention to sanitation, nutrition and other health services in several households,' said one person.

'Anyone else wants to share other experiences . . .?' Anuradha asked them. 'The field functionaries first.'

'I had a similar experience in a slum in east Delhi. In one *mohalla* parents refused to let their children receive the polio drops until the local government attended to other essential needs such as water, electricity, livelihoods . . .' said someone.

'Besides, amongst some communities, there are baseless rumours that polio drops are aimed at curbing population and will make their children sterile,' said yet another.

Anuradha was informed that suspicion and mistrust were exacerbated by the fact that some of the children had developed polio despite receiving multiple polio drops.

'Ma'am, that is a real tough one. The technical explanation is not convincing. What do you say to a family whose child fell victim to polio even though she was vaccinated against it multiple times? When I tried to find out why it happened in this case, I was told that children living in unsanitary conditions often have diarrhoeal episodes, and that is why the girl may not have retained the vaccine in her gut. How do I share this with the parents of the little girl who is disabled forever?'

'Even with fifteen years behind us, Ma'am, a large number of parents continue to refuse polio drops for their children outright. These children are missed out in every campaign—the same children . . .'

Anuradha listened to the shared experiences from the field with consternation. The combined response of the team was incredible and formed the basis of a new strategy to make India polio free.

Historically, the key measure of performance had been 'the number of children reached with the polio drops in every round'. The higher the coverage, the more successful the round. Ninety per cent coverage was considered a success. Anuradha pondered over everything she had gleaned during the brainstorming session, looked at the data in front of her, and then made a change in the strategy that later proved to be the game changer. She turned the historical monitoring indicator on its head and started to review different indices. She also asked different questions:

'How many children have we missed in this round?'

'How many households refused vaccination—and why?'

'How many households have we not been able to reach in this round—and why?'

'Where exactly are the children and the households we missed?'

For fifteen years, the polio campaigns had been chasing the *number of vaccinations given* and also *the number of households and children covered.*

The programme had never before focused on tracking the children *not* covered, systematically, and the households *missed*, in the campaign.

The fact that the same child was being reached and vaccinated over and over again, while others were 'missed' or 'left out', had never quite been taken into account. Children who missed the first round of vaccinations continued to miss them consistently, despite multiple vaccination campaigns!

Furthermore, there had been no follow-up on the households that had refused vaccinations due to rumours, or mistrust, or for other reasons. The campaigns had also failed to shine light on the hotspots that the programme was unable to identify and reach.

All this changed with the new strategy. The focus shifted to making special efforts to reach the children and the households that had been left out in the previous round for whatever reason. The shift in focus was apparently simple and commonsensical. However, the outcome of these probing questions and the reformed matrix was profound.

'Missed child' took centre stage. Reaching every missed child was the new mantra. Anuradha reached an agreement with the NPSP that they would provide the requisite information on the 'missed children' within three days of the conclusion of each Pulse Polio round. Given they had never done this kind of analysis in the past, the NPSP struggled to keep their commitment. Anuradha would call the NPSP, without fail, on the fourth day of every round, to review the data and put together a follow-up strategy. The NPSP was under unrelenting pressure to gather data from all the states. Each state officer, in turn, had to make sure that every district reported the information on the 'missed children' and why they were not reached, in a systematic manner. It was a huge challenge. But the effort was worthwhile.

Accountability for reaching every missed child was duly fixed. A detailed analysis of the data was done at the ministry level. The analysis proved both useful and insightful with regard to specific interventions and the next course of action. Through an analysis of the data collected as per the new strategy, Anuradha realized how mistaken she herself had been as Haryana's Health Secretary a year earlier. On scrutinizing the data for Mewat, a high-risk district for polio, she was surprised to find that 400 households had refused polio drops in the Pulse Polio round. She recalled that two years earlier, as the Health Secretary, Haryana, she had led an aggressive vaccination drive and had been convinced—obviously incorrectly, from the data that lay before her—that there had been complete adoption of the polio vaccine in the region.

Information regarding the 'missed children' had neither been collated nor followed up for any kind of remedial action prior to 2010. This had led to potential hotspots of the virus going unnoticed. In the absence of a laser sharp-focus on the 'missed children' and their households, the 'refusal' by the community in Mewat would have continued and new polio cases would have flared up. Armed with specific data, Anuradha was able to liaise with the new Health Secretary of Haryana to help address the gaps in coverage. Local community influencers in Mewat were brought on board to administer polio drops to the children in the identified cluster of households that had hitherto refused to vaccinate their children.

Similar exercises were undertaken across all the states and hotspots were identified district-wise. The data pinpointed areas where a substantial number of children had been 'missed' and helped to unravel the reasons behind it, based on which remedial actions were suggested.

In some instances, the ground reports revealed that the Collectors had not convened meetings of the District Task Force, which had weakened the momentum. Anuradha interacted with the Collectors directly, even though it was not customary for a Joint Secretary in a central ministry to do so. She wrote to the Collectors across the country— applauding those who were leading effectively, and goading others who needed to be more vigilant. This small action unleashed a new energy in the field. Collectors no longer saw Pulse Polio as a routine government programme, but rather as a national priority in which they had to play a pivotal role. They started searching for the 'missed children' in their districts proactively, and firmly addressed the hesitancy and refusal of the parents to vaccinate their children. Community leaders played an active part in dispelling rumours and doubts.

Sophisticated environmental surveillance was intensified in the big cities, with the support of the NPSP. This entailed taking sewage samples to detect the wild polio virus. Delhi, Mumbai, and other metropolitan cities, with a mushrooming slum population, were at a high risk of having a concentration of missed children. Environmental surveillance helped to identify urban clusters where the virus was still lurking, and highlighted the polio hotspots.

Over 40,00,00 high-risk communities were identified: urban slums, migrants, families who worked at brick kilns and on construction sites, and communities that lived away from habitation. In these hotspots, routine immunization services provided by the Health Ministry were strengthened, as the concerned populations were at risk not only for polio but also for other vaccine-preventable diseases.

'Missed' communities were also an embodiment of compounded vulnerabilities, requiring multi-sectoral interventions. Besides a high incidence of infectious diseases, these high-risk neighbourhoods had unacceptable rates of maternal and child mortality. They lacked access to basic sanitation as well as personal hygiene. Children were often malnourished and were not enrolled in school. Girls were particularly vulnerable and often victims to early marriage, domestic violence and lack of access to contraception and skilled birth attendance. In addition, they suffered from high levels of anemia and low agency.

Anuradha seized opportunities for integration. This helped to foster trust and rapport with the communities. Through an integrated approach, multiple health enhancing interventions were bundled together for co-delivery. The aim was to enhance awareness and improve health-seeking behaviour, which would help not only polio eradication but broader public-health outcomes.

The novel strategy of measuring gaps in the coverage, understanding the reasons for the gap, and making concerted remedial efforts on a war footing, was bolstered by a technological breakthrough in 2010. The bivalent oral polio vaccine was developed. India planned to be the first country to introduce the newly developed bivalent vaccine, which could concurrently build immunity against both the P1 and P3 strains of the wild polio virus. The bivalent vaccine was the answer to the problematic outcomes of the existing monovalent oral polio vaccines. It also dispensed with the necessity to administer two monovalent vaccines.

For several years, the monovalent vaccines had proved to be suboptimal. The use of the monovalent P1 vaccine tended to push up P3 cases, while the use of the monovalent P3 vaccine increased the number of P1 cases. With the discovery of the new bivalent vaccine, hopes were riding high.

During a review meeting, Anuradha smiled at her team as she shared the positive results filtering in with the Health Secretary. 'Our strategy is working. Polio cases are coming down and our goal to make India polio free is finally in sight.'

'Good. Knock on wood,' the Secretary replied a bit too soon, for the very next week, Anuradha and her team ran into a major problem.

India's global tender for the bivalent polio vaccine failed. All the three WHO-prequalified global manufactures of the vaccine that had bid for the tender were delisted, following a quality audit. The vaccines used during the Pulse Polio campaigns were being funded with a loan from the World Bank. The rules of the World Bank required all the vaccines to be procured from the manufacturers prequalified by WHO. An Indian company had also bid for the global tender, and was manufacturing the bivalent vaccine in India. The company had already been approved by the National Regulatory Agency. However, it had not yet obtained prequalification by WHO. There was also no likelihood of the organization prequalifying a manufacturer any time soon.

Options were running out—and time was of vital importance. Purchasing the vaccine from the Indian company meant a loss of funding from the World Bank due to their stringent rules. Not purchasing the vaccine from the Indian source meant that India would not be able to introduce the bivalent vaccine for several months. The latter would have been a terrible option for a country on the threshold of an exciting new era. Anuradha was in a dilemma.

'For our national immunization programme, the Universal Imminization Programme (UIP), we procure our vaccines—including the polio vaccines—from this company and also from several other Indian manufacturers approved by our NRA, don't we?' she thought. She scrutinized the purchase procedures, the approval process, and the regulatory environment of NRA—and compared them with those of WHO. 'Our NRA has robust regulatory processes comparable with WHO—the reason why it is duly certified by WHO.' She continued to reason with herself. 'Now, logically, since India's NRA is approved by WHO, then it follows that all the vaccines approved by NRA meet the quality standards as per WHO requirements.'

Under the national UIP, the Health Ministry procured vaccines from the NRA-approved manufacturers. All vaccines so procured, including those against polio, were of good quality and effective. Ironically, polio vaccines procured from the NRA-approved manufacturers, for the same population during the same period, were not allowed to be purchased for the World Bank-funded Pulse Polio campaigns. Instead, for the latter, the vaccines were procured from the WHO-prequalified manufacturers only—and at a much higher cost.

Anuradha walked into the office of Naved Masood the Financial Adviser (FA), in the Ministry of Health. 'Sir, I need your support . . . to ensure that our polio eradication initiative succeeds.' She explained her predicament and paused before she argued her point of view. 'I find it difficult to comprehend the logic, sir. A vaccine from an NRA-approved manufacturer is efficacious against polio when it's domestically funded under the UIP. Why should the same vaccine from the same manufacturer lose its efficacy against the same disease only because the source of funding is the World Bank?'

Dr Masood laughed as he said, 'Indeed. We need to correct that anomaly.'

'Would you please give me additional domestic budget to procure the bivalent vaccine, sir? Introducing it is critical at this juncture in our battle against polio.'

'Purchasing the polio vaccine, with the same objective and efficacy, from different sources at different rates is not prudent. I'm surprised, Anuradha, that no one ever raised this issue.'

Dr Masood was a man of high integrity with a deep passion for development. He needed no further convincing. He thought for a moment, scrutinized the overall budget of the ministry and smiled as he looked up. 'I see some savings and unspent balance in another project this year. Go ahead . . . Send me the proposal along with the justifications, on a file, and you will have the budget approval the same day.'

Very few officers would have stuck their necks out in this manner, especially where a financial transaction was involved. Most would have simply played safe and covered their backs by tendering again and again to ensure that no one ever questioned their credentials.

Both Dr Masood and Anuradha were made of sterner stuff. In placing the order at an NRA-approved manufacturer, who did not meet the World Bank conditions, thereby losing out on the World Bank loan—and allocating alternative unutilized domestic funding to the cause, which would have lapsed otherwise—the Financial Adviser and the Joint Secretary had taken a decision, which was quite out of the ordinary. The driving force behind their choice—which later proved to be life-altering—was the knowledge that every day lost meant the exposure of more and more children to the deadly polio virus.

They were in a position to make a difference—and both of them cared enough to do so, fully aware that it could be called to question at a later date. As a result, India became the first country in the world to roll out the bivalent polio vaccine successfully.

All the 'missed' children were followed up rigorously until every child, everywhere in the country, had received the two drops of life. The task was no longer limited to conducting multiple Pulse Polio rounds as stand-alone exercises. Each round was used as the beginning of an opportunity to detect unreached households. This was followed by continuing engagement outside the Pulse Polio round to build and sustain trust.

In the last lap of the polio marathon, the new paradigm shift yielded huge dividends and made it possible to step closer to the goal of universal polio vaccination. The country sailed through the high-transmission season. Surveillance continued to be of top quality. Environmental samples no longer showed the wild polio virus in the sewage.

Just as the reports across the country started giving rise to the belief that India had covered the last inch, there was another major setback. In January 2011, during a period of low-risk transmission, the virus struck—and that too at a place which was not a hotspot. The team led by Anuradha was dismayed, but also deeply worried. Howrah, the hometown of Rukhsar, the polio-afflicted child, was very densely populated, and the virus could spread in the area at lightning speed. There was not a minute to lose.

Anuradha convened a meeting with her team and technical partners to plan for a 'snap interruption' of the transmission.

'Typically, it takes a couple of weeks for an emergency mop up,' said her team.

'It requires special rounds of polio immunization for lakhs of children living in the surrounding areas.'

Once the reasons cited for why the mop-up process would take so long had been evaluated, simultaneous steps required to cut out delays became clearer. A critical path was identified to speed up the vaccine supply for the mop-up. The state authorities were involved to ensure social mobilization and logistics in a parallel rather than sequential manner to save time.

'Let's begin right away. We all have understood how we can manage all the different complexities of the process. It has to be done within five days—and not a day longer. Let's get going,' said Anuradha, instilling enthusiasm in her team.

The Indian Howrah mop-up happened on the sixth day. Globally, it is cited as the fastest ever!

'Why did the Howrah case happen if the programme was succeeding in reaching every child?' —was the question Anuradha and her team sought answers to even before the mop-up was over.

Apparently, a cluster of unvaccinated children had not been detected in time. No cure could be offered to Rukhsar. However, the enthusiastic health team was even more determined to ensure that no other child was 'missed' in any part of the country. A strong signal was sent out that attaining 'zero' polio cases was non-negotiable.

In April 2011, Anuradha persuaded the Union Health Minister to take a rather unique step and declare polio as a Public Health Emergency. All states and union territories were on high alert. An Emergency Preparedness and

Response Plan (EPRP) was put in place, and a 200-strong Rapid Response Team stood ready to act at all times. The next one year was marked by an alert vigil to ensure that the virus did not raise its ugly head again. The long-cherished dream of a full year of zero-polio-cases finally came true on 13 January 2012. History had been made. A month later, the WHO took India off the list of polio-endemic countries.

There was both jubilation and disbelief around the world. Globally, India's success in reaching zero-polio cases was acclaimed as one of the greatest public-health feats. The International Monitoring Board was incredulous, and full of praise for India's stunning victory over the obdurate wild polio virus. Millions of health workers, volunteers, parents, social mobilizers, influencers and technical partners, were proud of the achievement. Their tireless efforts had led to this incredible success.

Several high-level delegations from nations still struggling with polio—Pakistan, Nigeria and Afghanistan—visited India to understand how the country had reduced its polio cases to zero in such a short period, a little over a year, when the goal of a polio-free country had been elusive for so long despite great expenditure.

At the Global Vaccine Summit, Anuradha's team received a standing ovation to celebrate India's unique achievement. She was both enthralled and humbled by the success, but was reluctant to declare victory. Reaching 'zero polio cases' had been daunting, but sustaining 'zero polio cases' was even more formidable!

India needed to maintain the zero-polio status for another two years for complete eradication. Anuradha was aware that the slightest complacency at that stage could bring the demonic virus back. Her constant message to her team and the states was to not drop guard, and to remain focused on ensuring that not even a single child was missed across the country.

What worried her most was the high risk of importation of the polio virus from Pakistan, India's neighbour. Pakistan had experienced a spike in polio cases around that time. It was time to act swiftly. WHO's International Health Regulations (IHRs), permitted travel restrictions between countries with a view to prevent the spread of communicable diseases from one to the other.

Anuradha sought to invoke the IHRs to prevent ingress from Pakistan. This was an unprecedented demand. Margaret Chang, the then Director General of WHO, was aghast. 'The International Health Regulations are there, but they have never ever been invoked by any country!' she exclaimed.

Anuradha was determined. She was convinced that the hard-won gains would be lost if a single infected child from Pakistan entered India. Convincing the Union Health Minister was the easy part. The Ministry of External Affairs (MEA) was reluctant to consider the health ministry's proposal to mandate, and provide, polio drops to every child entering India from Pakistan. Given the diplomatic environment, the MEA was concerned about the ramifications of such a measure.

Fortunately, Anuradha found a believer in her counterpart in the MEA, A. R. Ghanashyam, a senior Indian Foreign Service (IFS) officer. Her passionate plea resonated with him, and he was completely persuaded by the time she finished explaining the consequences of not going ahead with her proposal.

'God only knows how much time, effort, and money India will need to become polio free again if we allow access from Pakistan now. And what about our children? They would be potential victims due to the unchecked passage,' she sighed.

Ghanashyam was convinced that it was the right thing to do in national interest.

'Luck is definitely favouring me,' she thought as she put down the phone after a long discussion with him.

From then onwards, Ghanashyam was the prime advocate for the cause and took the battle forward within the MEA—based on stimulating exchanges of information with Anuradha, mostly through SMS messages, in the midst of myriad meetings.

Many within the MEA vehemently opposed the proposal. India's Ambassador to Pakistan fought it tooth and nail. Every time some important person within the MEA raised an objection, Ghanashyam promptly relayed it to Anuradha. At her end, she provided him with more information and ammunition to counter the argument. It was a long battle of nerves.

India's Foreign Secretary at that time was a very brave woman. Overlooking all the arguments by several MEA officers, she approved the Ministry of Health's proposal at her own level—without even referring the matter to the Minister of External Affairs. A notification was issued to Indian Missions in Pakistan. Polio vaccination facilities were set up at the Missions so that polio drops could be given at the time of granting the visa. The Health Ministry also put systems in place to administer polio vaccinations at 102 locations along India's international border and entry points, including Wagha, for those entering India by rail or road.

There was quite an uproar in Pakistan. The diplomatic channels were strained. As many as forty-nine countries that were polio-free had suffered from polio virus importations. That India remained free of polio despite continuing travel from Pakistan, even against an increase in polio cases in that country, and a few others, was a vindication of the unusual and bold steps taken just in time.

The polio fighters remained undeterred. One day after their collective mission was accomplished, Ghanashyam dropped in to see Anuradha at her office. They had talked incessantly over the phone, and passed thousands of messages during their combined battle, but had never met each other even once.

'I just wanted to put a face to the name. I wanted to see how you look in real life,' Ghanashyam said with a laugh as they shared a celebratory coffee.

The tribulations, however, were not yet over. Though India was no longer polio endemic, Anuradha kept an eye on the Emergency Preparedness & Response Plan (EPRP), which was updated constantly. The exigency plan laid down detailed steps for the course of action in the event of any future indigenous or imported wild polio case.

The efficacy of the exigency plan was put to test soon enough—in October 2012. A wild polio case was reported from Darbhanga in Bihar. The entire team was despondent. Anuradha felt as if somebody had sucked all the energy out of her.

'How can all our efforts come to naught?' she wondered.

She instantaneously convened a meeting of all the stakeholders and, as per the EPRP protocol, a media release was sent out. Liaising with the State Health Secretary, a surgical mop-up was planned and conducted in Bihar, along the lines of the Howrah episode. For three days the ministry was in a state of consternation. On the fourth day, Dr Deshpande, Director of the Virology Lab that had tested the stool sample, called up to convey news that raised everyone's spirits again.

'Madam, the Darbhanga case is not a case of wild polio.'

'Really?' Anuradha was incredulous. 'But didn't the stool sample test positive?'

'Yes, madam, it did. I am sorry, but it seems that the sample was contaminated in the lab where it was first tested. We have just finished the genetic sequencing. It was a false alarm.'

As she put the phone down, Anuradha was smiling from ear to ear. She called her team in to let them know and to share her joy. India's success against the dreadful disease was intact and their efforts had proven foolproof.

The false alarm had one positive outcome—it tested the ministry's emergency preparedness. The Darbhanga event was construed as a 'simulation exercise' and demonstrated India's capacity to respond at record speed within four days. The protocols of India's EPRP proved to be both efficacious and flawless. The plan and preparedness were commended globally.

That was the last time India ever heard of a case of wild polio—real or false. The future generations of children in India are now safe, and the nation is protected against acute flaccid paralysis caused by the virulent polio virus.

Coda

After three years of zero polio cases, India celebrated polio eradication in January 2014. The country remained untouched by the increasing number of polio outbreaks across the world in 2013, including countries that had not seen the virus in years. It completed two years of zero polio that year. India's victory against polio continues to be a story of national and international curiosity and interest.

The Global Polio Eradication Initiative is ongoing. India's experience offered unique lessons for Pakistan, Afghanistan and Nigeria, which continued to witness a spike in polio cases. Nigeria has recently been declared free from polio, but Pakistan and Afghanistan are still fighting the scourge. The global finishing line appears further still.

During her tenure with the government of India, Anuradha was later promoted as Additional Secretary and mission director of the National Rural Health Mission. This broadened the scope of her work. She helped India nearly attain the Millennium Development Goals (MDGs) on maternal and child survival through creative and strategic planning. She also started a national initiative of universal screening of children to detect defects at birth, diseases, deficiencies and development delays. Intervention centres were set up for follow-up support. The wellness approach for adolescents was widened to include self-harm, psychological disorders, gender-based violence, obesity, nutritional disorders and substance abuse.

Besides polio, Anuradha helped to universalize the Hepatitis B vaccination and introduce the pentavalent vaccine, overcoming vexatious litigation and false propaganda by the anti-vaccine lobby in India. Anemia—an omnipresent public health issue in India—was attacked through a targeted programme.

At present Anuradha is in Geneva as the deputy chief executive officer of GAVI—with a mission of expanding access to life-saving vaccines in seventy-three lower-income countries. GAVI is a unique alliance of UN agencies, donors, countries, private sectors and civil societies, set up in 2000. Here, Anuradha has ventured into innovative financing mechanisms like vaccine bonds to raise billions of dollars on the capital market, shaping vaccine markets through the pooling of vaccine demand for 60 per cent of the world's children, and leveraging volumes and predictable financing.

Anuradha remains a champion of differentiated, country-specific and contextual approaches—driving a paradigm shift at the global level. Her versatile India experience has proved to be of great value in GAVI's aim to close the global immunization gap, and reach those 11,00,00,00 children who remain deprived of even a single shot of the most basic life-saving vaccines. Preventing deaths and protecting generations is her passion and mission.

In a world turned upside down by Covid-19, GAVI is at the forefront to find a way out of the pandemic in an attempt to ensure equitable access to Covid-19 vaccines and the mitigation of its disruptive impact on childhood immunization. Anuradha is an important part of its initiative on this front.

III

Power of the People

From doubt to trust, and ignorance to light,
from hatred to love, and the dismal to the bright
a path that meanders along a meaningful life . .

'Anita Kaul had an unshakeable faith in the power of ordinary people—in teachers, literacy volunteers, social activists and children—to bring a momentous change in their own lives and the lives of others,' said someone.

'She drew her inspiration from ordinary people, and had a firm belief in Constitutional values and an inclusive society,' said someone else.

'Anita was committed to the Constitution of India, but not aligned to any one government or political party,' said Anita's minister.

'What a perfectionist she was! She was quite the artist. But, unlike an artist, she put her trust in collaborations and in joining hands,' said her colleague.

As the sun went down on that October evening, in 2016, Rohan sat listening to strangers and friends shower accolades on Anita Kaul five days after she had passed away. The hall, where the memorial meeting was being held, overflowed with well-wishers from far and wide. The tributes kept pouring in from people with diverse backgrounds: seniors like Laxmidhar Mishra and Anshu Vaish; batchmates and friends like Anuradha Rajivan, Kusumjit Sidhu, and Sobha Nambisan; junior colleagues like T.R. Raghunandan, I.S.N. Prasad, and Vandita who had become friends over the years; members of civil society like Krishna Kumar and T. Sundararaman from B.G.V.S., and S. Sudha Sundararaman—a leader of the women's movement; film-makers such as Deepa Dhanraj; theatre activists and poets such as Laxmi Krishnamurthy, Prasanna and Kotiganahalli Ramaiah; schoolteachers and education officers such as Latif, Gayathri and Baig; educationists such as Prof. Krishna Kumar, Vimala Ramachandran and Anita Rampal.

'I saw her throw hierarchy to the winds!'

'She touched many minds and hearts—as no other officer had.'

'A sunny temperament, a commitment to egalitarian partnerships . . . and humility!'

'Hardworking, insightful, empathetic and deeply committed.'

The eulogies kept coming. Rohan pondered over all that was being said, and over Anita's many incredible facets. His thoughts went back to the day twenty years ago when the nine-year-old boy had tried to understand why his mother was dressing him up in a drab black gown with letters in the

Devanagari script while his friend, Abhay, had been bought a brand-new Superman suit in bright blue and red, for a fancy-dress competition at school.

'You, Rohan, are going as Saksharta Mission—the National Literacy Mission,' Anita explained.

'Maa, I don't like this plain black robe with *ka kha gha* pinned on it. Why can't I dress up like the others boys at school as Batman or Superman—or even Robin?'

'But, Rohan, you are dressed as the most powerful superhero of them all!'

'Maa! Fancy-dress competitions are about true superheroes! The sort with weapons like a sword or a batarang!'

'Son . . . *saksharta* [literacy] is the most powerful weapon to change the world.'

'Really? More powerful than Batman or Superman?' asked Rohan, incredulously.

'Yes. Way more powerful! If anyone asks, tell them that the Saksharta Mission will educate more than a 1,00,00,000 people in less than ten years. Saksharta will transform more lives than all the other superheroes in the world put together.'

Anita paused to pin a letter that had come off the costume.

'Next time I go to the field, I'll take you with me. You can see the "Saksharta superhero" in action for yourself, son.'

Anita sighed as Rohan left for his fancy-dress competition, and her thoughts went back to her own childhood. Having lost her father when she was not yet twelve, Anita had always idolized her older sister, Gita, who had taken on the mantle of a father, friend, and mentor. Their father, a government servant in the postal department, had died young and left some savings to provide his two daughters with a good education. In fact, it was education that ensured that the girls stood on their own feet and made a life for themselves. Gita, elder to Anita by six years, joined the Indian Revenue Service and motivated Anita to dream of a career more varied and gratifying than that of a German translator and travel guide— jobs she had taken up after finishing college. Even as she joined the Indian Administrative Service, Anita never forgot the role education had played in their lives to empower them to rise above adversity. Education remained Anita's passion—a passion she followed for most part of her career.

Bureaucrats are not supposed to be passionate about their work. It is believed that if you develop an attachment to your work, you allow your heart to rule over your head—and that is not supposed to be good for well-reasoned policymaking. Nor are bureaucrats supposed to disrupt hierarchy.

Anita did not quite fit the idea of an archetypal bureaucrat. She was rather passionate about reforms, change and education.

'Almost like an activist,' a colleague had once sneered. To Anita, that had been a beautiful compliment.

Within the bureaucracy Anita Kaul was known to possess the traits of an activist, and amongst the stakeholders and people at large, she was the medium through whom their issues would be heard and understood in the government circles. Once she decided to get something done, she would never give up, even though it was difficult to negotiate with the different levels of the government. She was always eager to solve the problem. She would go from desk to desk, argue her point of view and get that sluggish file moving. She was rather gentle but resolute. She was dedicated to her work, but was not aggressive.

The Chief Secretary of Karnataka had once said about her, 'She can make the chief ministers change their views with gentle persuasion.'

As for hierarchy, Anita simply did not believe in it. Anita Kaul, an officer from the 1979 batch, was from the Karnataka cadre. Out of a remarkable thirty-five-year career, she had spent twenty-two years in social sectors like education, nutrition, and policymaking related to women and children. Even when she was posted outside the social sectors, she was able to create space for bringing in innovations and a fresh approach to the assignment. As a matter of choice, a major portion of her career was spent in Education—both in Karnataka and in the Government of India.

Anita's long journey in the education sector began with her posting in the Government of India as Deputy Secretary (DS) in charge of the National Literacy Mission (NLM), and continued for her entire life. At the Ministry of Human Resource Development, she handled several programmes related to elementary education and literacy. She played a critical role in the passage of the Right of Children to Free and Compulsory Education or Right to Education (RTE) Act, 2009. Due to her reticence, not too many people are aware that she was one of the principal architects of the RTE Act, the consequential legislation under Article 21-A of the Constitution of India that made free and compulsory education a fundamental right for every child.

Anita never quite concerned herself with recognition or accolades even as she went beyond the call of duty to ensure that the legislation, despite several incarnations, remained true to its original values and principles. She collaborated and built consensus with large cross-sections, including civil society groups. She waged an uphill battle against the naysayers prior to the passage of the Bill—and a rather acrimonious legal one in the Supreme Court after the Act had been passed. Recognizing that education was a basic human right, the 2009 Act ensured the provision of inclusive elementary education to all, and heralded the dawn of a new set of opportunities for the children in India.

For Anita, the RTE was the logical pinnacle of a long journey that had begun two decades earlier. The uphill but gratifying voyage began on a foggy January morning in 1988 when Anita was appointed Deputy Secretary (DS, and later Director), National Literacy Mission (NLM), at the Ministry of Human Resource Development (HRD), Government of India, for about four years. Even before she joined service, she was informed that the Secretary Education, Anil Bordia, would like to see her in his chamber as soon as she had finished with her joining formalities.

He had the reputation of being a brilliant achiever and a hard taskmaster. It was said, 'If you survive four years with him, you are a special person—and have a *rishta* for life.'

Anita was both apprehensive and concerned. She was new to the sector and worried about why a secretary would want to bother with a Deputy secretary. In the scheme of things, a DS in GoI was a mere cog in the wheel—too small and insignificant for a Secretary to know—leave alone invite to his office the very day she joined the ministry. The prospect was rather daunting.

After sending her name on a slip of paper through the peon, Anita knocked on the door gingerly. She entered the Secretary's room with much unease. Anil Bordia stood before a blackboard with a chalk in his fingers, explaining an idea, or rather discussing it, with a group of about twelve people. Her anxiety must have been visible to the group huddled around a table in the centre of the room. He paused, indicated that she should join them, and introduced her to Lakshmidhar Mishra, Director General (DG), NLM, and the other officers in the ministry, including K.M. Acharya, Amitabh, Kiran Dhingra, Sukhdeep and Vimala, as 'the newest member of the education team'.

'Welcome, Anita. A pleasure to have you on Team NLM. Mishra will take a couple of days to bring you up to speed on the National Literacy Mission strategy, and how far it has reached. I hope you are prepared to work long hours and travel extensively across the length and breadth of India.'

Anita nodded in the affirmative, a little wide-eyed at her dynamic new boss.

'There is absolutely no time to lose. We are at the cusp of a great transformation—a change we need to bring about in a Mission mode.' Anil Bordia stopped pacing up and down and elaborated on it for Anita's benefit. 'The National Literacy Mission is about to adopt a systematically planned campaign approach to literacy through mass mobilization and innovative learning techniques that emphasize predetermined learning levels . . .'

He paused and picked up the slip Anita had sent in through the peon, on which she had neatly penned her name and designation and reason for visit as: 'official—to call on Secretary Education, MoHRD, GoI'.

'Anita, you are the newest member of the team that will be spearheading this revolution. Like the rest of the team, you have the freedom to walk into my room if you have any doubts or ideas or thoughts to share . . . and please don't bother with sending in a slip or using such formal language to address me.'

'Yes, sir. Thank you, sir,' Anita nodded.

The enthusiasm in the charged room was infectious. She felt a sense of admiration for her new boss, as well as responsibility and commitment towards the task at hand. As she left, she felt elated. She had expected that as Deputy Secretary, NLM, her work would entail dealing with a pile of faceless dusty files in a remote corner in the labyrinthine corridors of Shastri Bhavan—where one could lose one's way and identity at the same time. The NLM sounded exhilarating.

The team met Director General, NLM, and the Secretary, at 9.00 a.m. every Monday to strategize—and sometimes three or four times a week, whenever something important needed to be brainstormed, discussed or fleshed out. On one occasion, soon after Anita joined the ministry, the Secretary asked her whether she had settled down and how she liked the work.

'What have you been doing all morning?' he enquired.

'I was looking through some old files, sir,' Anita replied.

Anil Bordia laughed in a gentle manner. 'You don't learn about literacy campaigns through files. Come, let me show you . . .'

And then he showed Anita what she needed to see, as they travelled far and wide. She toured the country with the DG and the Secretary. She visited Baba Amte's Bharat Jodo Abhiyan in Mirzapur. She saw how the Secretary participated in the meetings of, and engaged with, the All India People's Science Network and the Bharat Gyan Vigyan Samiti. She accompanied him to Ernakulam, Burdwan, Midnapur, Pondicherry, Sikar, Jalna and Nellore. Wherever they went, the Secretary took great hope, confidence and optimism.

'Literacy will change people's lives—in more ways than one,' he said. 'And indeed it has already done so for many as you have seen for yourself, Anita. The women in Puddukkottai, who used their numeracy skills to win quarrying contracts and start gem cutting work; the women who participated in the anti-arrack campaign in Nellore and grew into a self-help group; the Mahila Swastha Sanghas in Jalna, who wove health issues into the literacy campaigns— participated in an experience that changed their lives forever.'

Anita saw, and absorbed, and learnt. And, with every passing day, her commitment towards literacy and education grew until it became a passion. A couple of months later, having travelled to remote villages and *mufasil* towns in Bihar, Rajasthan, Maharashtra, Andhra, Pondicherry and Kerala, she was bubbling with energy and was full of ideas at the 'Monday meeting'—ideas she needed to share with the team despite her reserve.

She said, 'I have just returned from Rohan—a village with a population of 1,400 in West Champaran district, Bihar. There is a problem that we all need to bring into focus . . . 50 per cent of the children of the village do not attend its primary school. When I delved deeper, I found that the proportion of out-of-school children poses a problem that urgently needs to be addressed.' She paused, saw that everyone was listening expectantly, and elaborated. 'You see, while all the children from upper-caste families, and lately those from agricultural communities like Yadava, Kurmis and Ahirs, attend school—the ones who do not, and those who drop out, belong to the families of schedule castes like Chamars, Bhangis, and Julahas and tribal families initially brought in as indentured labourers by the British indigo planters from south Bihar. There is a complex caste-based exclusion we need to address in policymaking. In my opinion, we can't look at universal literacy in a silo. We should broaden the NLM vision. We need to address the failure of the universalization of primary education along with the complex socio-economic issues and the issue of systemic discrimination in which such failure is grounded. Unless we ensure that primary education is available to all, the fresh flow of illiterates will never be arrested— and the National Literacy Mission will continue to fight a never-ending battle.'

The normally introverted Anita blushed as she looked around the table at the faces of her colleagues and seniors, who were surprised at her impassioned speech. She gave a shy grin and continued. 'You will agree that there can be no single blueprint for the universalization of basic education. I am convinced that it has to be contextual. The context varies from village to village, block to block, district to district, depending on the prevalent social, economic, political and cultural patterns. Besides, something else has been bothering me. I think that to truly improve the lives of the learners, we need to shift our focus from *one-time* literacy learning to *lifetime* education. I believe people's participation and collaborations with civil society and mass organizations is essential. Innovation and a bottom-up approach are what will work.'

'Great work, Anita. Clearly, what you have said has resonated deeply with all of us in the room. Some of these ideas need to be discussed more deeply. Welcome to the NLM, Anita—truly,' Anil Bordia said seriously, but with a warm smile.

And that was the beginning of a twenty-year-long association with a nurturing boss who encouraged his juniors to speak their minds and gave space for new ideas—a *rishta* built on mutual respect.

At the NLM, Anita was instrumental in taking the Total Literacy Campaigns (TLCs) from less than ten districts when she joined work, to close to a 100 districts later, by criss-crossing the country, energizing and motivating the Collectors, and often travelling twenty days in a month to remote corners of the country. Her zeal was anchored in the belief that the values of equality, social justice, democracy, and the creation of a just and humane society in India, were possible only through education.

'The delivery of education needs to be transferred from the hierarchy of officialdom to mass organizations. I think we need to recognize that literacy is not merely a "need", but also a "right" of the masses,' she said to her peers one summer evening in Birmalu, just as the Kala Jatha finished performing under the sky.

The NLM had started using Kala Jathas—folk theatre comprising no-frill plays of fifteen to thirty minutes, performed by groups of theatre artists—to generate awareness. The Jathas travelled from village to village, and district to district, to sing, dance and entertain. The arrival of a Kala Jatha in a village was met with a warm reception. After the performance, the theatre artists and volunteers would sit around chatting for long hours. The entire experience was enthralling.

The NLM team was on an official tour of Rajasthan. Birmalu was a small village in Jaipur district with a population of 600. That evening Anita was particularly moved by the Kala Jatha performance and the huge enthusiasm of the volunteers at the end of the show.

'When you say "right" of the masses, do you mean a justiciable right?' Anil Bordia asked her.

'I do, sir. I know this may not be the right time to talk about rights. We are still in the early stages of our Literacy Mission. But every Indian must have the right to education in line with Article 13 of the International Covenant on Economic, Social and Cultural Rights. Maybe one day education will become a fundamental right,' Anita replied.

'That's a good thought,' said Laxmidhar Mishra. 'Even the Acharya Ramamurti Committee has recommended the inclusion of right to education as a fundamental right rather than a mere directive principle of state policy in our Constitution. The state has an obligation to provide education and take steps to achieve education for all progressively, by appropriate means. But it's a tough call, given the constraints.'

'I agree with Anita. If education for all is to be a reality in India, we need to have a RTE Act that is justiciable,' Anil Bordia said sombrely. 'Recently, the Supreme Court has given several landmark judgments supporting the right to basic education, while examining the issue in the Mohini Jain case. A Constitutional amendment of Article 21 is required . . . and a new legislation too. Perhaps someday it will happen . . . It *has* to happen.'

Anita looked up at the stars. Somehow, they seemed brighter—with hope.

The seeds of the Right to Education legislation, enacted in 2009, were possibly sown on that star-filled night in the small village outside the capital of Rajasthan as the three committed officers and friends sat talking about a 'right to' rather than a 'need for' education.

The National Literacy Mission was also the crucible for an experiment very close to Anita's heart—an experiment in child-centric 'joyful learning', the efficacy of which is evident from the fact that it had a lasting impact on primary-school education, and continues to do so in Karnataka.

In November 1992, after working with the NLM for four years, Anita moved back to Karnataka. She worked as Joint- and later Additional Secretary in the Education Department for a year, followed by a few years on different assignments in the Secretariat, the Vidhan Soudha, in Bengaluru, where she left her mark. Her uniqueness lay in the manner in which the others reacted to her.

When most officers walked down the corridors of the Vidhana Soudha, peons, clerks and the others, who happened to be there at the same time, would shrink back into the shadows respectfully until the person had passed by. As Anita walked by, people would come forward with smiling faces to greet her with a namaste, and sometimes hold her hand

and ask, *'Hegideera* Madam? *Chennagideera*? [How are you, madam? I hope you are well?]'

Education brought Anita back into its folds in May 1996. She was posted as Project Director (PD), Karnataka, District Primary Education Programme (DPEP) for almost four years as Secretary of the state, Primary and Secondary Education. This was the period when she actualized her dreams—Nali Kali.

A student-centred system of learning, assessment, and classroom management for primary schools, Nali Kali started in 1995, as a small UNICEF-assisted pilot project in HD Kote, Mysore, but became a reality under Anita's vision and insight through the DPEP in Karnataka. From a search for means to revitalize the primary schools, starting with a visit of fifteen teachers to the Rishi Valley satellite schools, Nali Kali gradually expanded to 270 schools in Mysore between 1995–96, 4,000 schools in the districts of Mysore, Mandya, Kolar, Raichur and Belgaum by 1998, and soon became a statewide movement under the DPEP. The pedagogical innovations of the DPEP during this period were heralded as 'little short of a renaissance' in the development of Indian education.

Joyful learning through a child-friendly curriculum and delivery system was at the core of Nali Kali. Primary school teachers were deeply involved with the curriculum and were made responsible for preparing the content. Enthused teachers designed and developed high-quality content. In gentle ways, Anita was able to push for gender equity and empowerment, including in the type of learning materials developed—which were prepared locally to enable each child to learn at their own pace. She had utmost faith and confidence in the capability of the teachers. Nali Kali had a prudent holistic approach.

Anita's experience with the NLM helped broaden the scope and effectiveness of Nali Kali. She was convinced that a one-shoe-fits-all model would not work. Therefore, a certain level of flexibility was built into the content, and even the school calendar and timings, taking into consideration locally prevalent agricultural, geographical, climatic and cultural patterns. If a child was absent from school, for whatever reason, she was able to join where she had left off. Several aspects of the universalization of primary education were addressed. Child-centric learning, trained teachers, faith in the teachers' ability to innovate, academic support and monitoring rather than 'inspections', better infrastructure and community management, were essential elements of the strategy. The tactic was rather unique and the approach remarkable at that time.

Education in India was—and still largely is—characterized by highly stratified hierarchical administrative structures and systems, as well as rigid, stereotyped, textbook-centric and teacher-dominated classroom transactions. The problems of first-generation schoolgoers are rarely factored into the curriculum. The traditional school calendar is inflexible and fixed to suit the convenience of education administrators. As a result, children are often absent and the overall learning at primary levels is low. The classroom-management system is authoritative, divisive and teacher-centric. The curriculum is drab, rigid, encourages rote learning and stifles creativity. The atmosphere is threatening and provides a poor foundation for learning at higher levels.

The task was overwhelming and there were several bottlenecks. The list of non-believers was never-ending. Many of the non-believers mattered, and included those who were to deliver Nali Kali. Many within the government were wary of change. There were also many naysayers, whose opinion was important. Pedagogy pundits had no faith in the capabilities of primary school teachers to prepare the curriculum, content, and learning material. Teachers themselves lacked self-confidence and required extensive training. Bureaucrats were wary of peoples' participation. Activists did not quite trust the government. Cynical parents were unhappy with the replacement of textbooks by learning cards, and also wanted to know why no homework was given to the children under the new system. Anita believed in the innate strength of the new system—and Nali Kali proved the naysayers wrong.

Always one to lead by example, Anita rose to the occasion—often at great cost to herself in terms of time and energy. She did more than she was expected to do. She travelled a great deal from one village to another across the state. She would arrive at schools and workshops, and sit unobtrusively amongst the teachers to understand their concerns, absorb them and strategize. She would be sitting cross-legged on the floor, listening—rather than issuing diktats.

Early into her tenure at the DPEP, Anita arrived unannounced at a workshop of schoolteachers being coordinated by MN Baig at Shravanbelagola in Hassan district. Baig, who later became a friend, had never seen Anita before. He was struck by her simplicity and unassuming manner. She arrived without any fanfare, sat down on the floor along with the primary school teachers, very inconspicuously, observing the entire process.

'Director Madam! Sorry, madam! We did not recognize you. We would have made arrangements . . .' Baig gasped once he learnt that the woman in the starched cotton sari, sitting on the floor to his right was, in fact, the PD, DPEP, Karnataka.

'Let me get a chair, madam . . .' said a teacher, rushing out of the room, before Anita could stop him.

The entire group was awestruck as they watched a most unusual IAS officer, who had spent an entire day with primary school teachers—sitting on the floor, listening to them, eating off a banana leaf—without expecting any special treatment. At the end of the workshop, when asked to say a few words, she spoke from the heart: 'This has been a wonderful learning experience for me. You have been *my* teachers today. I have great respect for you and the commitment with which you work under difficult conditions and despite all odds. I am convinced that teachers are not to be blamed for the ills of the Education Department. The key to our new approach will be *you*—the teachers,' she paused and smiled. 'Given time and space, I am convinced each one of you can design better, more effective and more creative teaching material than some of our eminent academicians. I am convinced that that you will be our strength—the strength of Nali Kali.'

Baig and the rest of the group, who heard Anita speak that day in Shravanbelagola in 1996, were struck by the conviction in her voice and the light in her eyes.

As she addressed group after group of schoolteachers in villages and towns across the state, she often said, 'We need to change the way our children experience school—how they learn in Nali Kali classrooms. Rather than an authoritarian figure or a "controller" of classroom activities, the role of a teacher will be that of a friendly and creative "facilitator". The curriculum, learning material and content, *has* to be local-specific. We will train you regarding "how to", but *you* will prepare it, test it and use it. Your class will be taught the learning material you prepare! Please ensure that the content is activity-based and the learning both interactive and joyful. Let us all initiate a process of innovation to make learning truly fun-filled, outcome-oriented and suited to each child's pace of learning.'

Anita trusted the primary school teachers. And the teachers trusted Anita. She was one of them. Together, they all made child-centric learning through Nali Kali a reality. Nali Kali prospered in Karnataka because the local administrators provided the space and the time for the teachers to question the existing pedagogical- and classroom-management practices.

During this period, the Commissioner of Public Instruction (CPI), Karnataka, was Sanjay Kaul, Anita's husband and batchmate. Both of them had a shared interest in education, but they had distinct working styles. While Sanjay was the typical bureaucrat and focused on issues such as transparency and reforms that were more conventional in the government space, Anita went beyond in reimagining the government as an instrument of social change.

The CPI and the PD, DPEP, of the state, had diverse views on several issues. In their approach to education, Sanjay was more mainstream and risk-averse, while Anita was a great believer in innovation and grounded in the philosophy of a collaborative approach involving those from the lowest strata. She had some radical views and, in some respects, was more of a social activist rather than a typical civil servant. Sanjay, on the other hand, was often sceptical about education through people's mobilization.

'So, I agree there are problems within the government space, but how does the creation of a "movement" help in education?' Sanjay asked, willing to admit that he was possibly hesitant because he did not have a full understanding of working at the grassroots.

'Actually, Sanjay, micro-planning and community-mobilization techniques can be adapted to enable people to question the education system. Mobilization can empower them to seek better educational services. And, if this goes hand-in-hand with the political and administrative will to improve learning, teaching-learning materials, evaluation processes, and classroom-management systems, I'm pretty sure that the universal basic education will become a reality.'

Their discussions were intense but healthy, forcing both to think through their opinions in a more cogent manner. They often ended up meeting on a common ground.

Late one evening, after returning from a hectic tour of three villages, Anita shared her concerns with Sanjay. 'Nali Kali is important. Learning has to be joyful. Our school system simply has to move away from the current control-from-the-top and "inspectorial" approach to one that is child-centric. We need to make primary school less threatening to a child. Something needs to be done about the existing evaluation system. You need to help us with this, Sanjay. I am very apprehensive about testing children and shifting all the blame to the teacher. All children should be able to learn at their own pace, without the fear of failure.' She sipped a cup of hot tea without milk—her favourite drink.

'I agree with you, Anita. We need to provide a non-threatening and affirming environment, but how can you do away with assessment? How do you intend to judge learning outcomes?' Sanjay asked her. 'If the Nali Kali approach has to be accepted across the board, there has to be some objective measure by which children are maintained at an age-appropriate pace of learning. Shouldn't there be a system to ensure that children who go up from class three have achieved class–three competencies'?

'Not necessarily. When we talk about the learning continuum, and that each child should learn at her own pace, then external evaluations go against the very spirit of Nali Kali. Evaluation has to be ongoing and non-threatening. In fact, children shouldn't even be aware they are being assessed. We are working on an evaluation system that makes them free of fear, trauma and anxiety—one that will help them to be more curious and to express their views freely.'

'But this is going to be incredibly difficult to achieve, given the demands it places on the teacher. The primary school teachers in government schools are possibly the least motivated functionaries in the state.' Sanjay expressed genuine concern.

'I know. And I fully recognize the challenges. A Nali Kali teacher has to be hands-on, on her toes—and alert all the time. Since a teacher will "own" the teaching material she herself has prepared, she can easily junk it if it doesn't work, or redesign it based on the reactions of the children in the classroom. Once a teacher realizes her own potential, it will truly be an empowering experience and one that transforms her into an educator.'

'That sounds right. But you will have to work really hard with them.'

'I know, Sanjay. It will be an uphill task. But, I am not in favour of formal testing for measuring learning outcomes. The key, as I see it, is to have a child-centred pedagogy, and a curriculum that will encourage continuous assessment by the teachers and the children themselves. We are working towards that and other things. There is so much to do—and at so many different levels,' Anita sighed. 'I still have to figure out the extent of peoples' participation—the roles and responsibilities—in the school-management committees. And another matter really bothers me. Somehow we need to recognize and value the native pre-knowledge of first-time schoolgoers and build upon that knowledge. I don't know what we can do right now. But, all children, irrespective of caste, gender and religion, come to school with this knowledge. It would really enhance their confidence and self-esteem.'

The CPI may not have agreed with the PD, DPEP, on all matters, and remained sceptical about the practicality of fully replacing textbooks with other material, but he respected her views—and also began to recognize the relevance of her approach later.

The approach in Nali Kali was indeed unique. The methodology had sizeable strengths. It promoted joyful learning as it was 'child-effort' rather than 'teacher-instruction'-oriented. Each child learnt at their own pace. The curriculum was seen as a continuum to be learnt over four years—and not compartmentalized into class-wise content areas. Textbooks were not central to learning. The education kit consisted of a series of carefully graded cards for language, mathematics and environmental studies. Children learnt through an interactive process, using a learning ladder and learning cards. Blank spaces in the ladder allowed the teachers to introduce independent content into the learning process. A child could re-enter the learning ladder at the point where she had left off. The content was broken down into small capsules. Learning cards were supplemented with puppetry, songs, village surveys, nature walks and other outdoor activities.

Pedagogic renewal in primary schools was at the heart of Nali Kali. Changes in the learning material and content were possible because of the card system, where the material was prepared locally and renewed by the teachers themselves. Even today, a Nali Kali classroom is a joyful, democratic and non-threatening space.

There was a cheerful buzz of activity—with none of the 'fingers-on-your-lips' and 'a-quiet-classroom-is-a-hardworking-classroom' stereotypes, typical of a traditional classroom. The children were organized into groups on the basis of the type of activity they were involved in—irrespective of age, level, ability, gender, caste or religion. They included the teacher-assisted group—for students embarking on a new unit, the peer-assisted group—in which more advanced students assisted the new entrants, and self learners—who worked on their own. The teachers moved from one group to another, encouraging the children to learn. The democratic classroom-management system, while allowing the children the freedom to learn at their own pace, also challenged caste and gender exclusionary group formations and encouraged cooperation. Children learnt to be self-reliant as they read, solved arithmetic problems and sang and danced with abandon.

The evaluation system was built into the learning process in a manner that did not build up stress or intimidate a child. Children were unaware that they were being evaluated. In fact, evaluation through games like 'Aasha atta' was part of the daily routine, making tests a painless experience for them.

Nali Kali also challenged the existing hegemony of the pedagogy pundits. In Karnataka, before Nali Kali, only eminent academicians and high-school teachers were considered competent enough to develop textbooks and teaching material for primary schools, by the Department of School Education Research and Training (DSERT). The content so prepared was often far removed from ground reality and sometimes age-inappropriate. Nali Kali changed the perception of the DSERT with regard to the competence of primary school government teachers. Materials, including workbooks, were developed through Nali Kali. Now the DSERT chiefly uses government primary schoolteachers for content development. Nali Kali has built a lasting legacy in the form of professional resource teams of primary school teachers for curriculum and content development in Karnataka.

Besides this, Nali Kali made several lasting contributions. In the larger context of DPEP in India, innovations like

Nali Kali in the state of Karnataka, demonstrated that there was much more to education than bricks, mortar and infrastructure—or even textbooks for that matter. A good, motivated teacher in an energized classroom could do wonders. Joyful learning ensured, among other things, the power of retention in the children, better learning outcomes, and it enhanced creativity. It also provided a stimulating atmosphere that promoted child-centric learning.

Since 2000, the Nali Kali reform has been studied extensively in India and abroad, and it has provided striking insights into how schools can deal more sensitively and effectively with persisting issues of social inequality and exclusion. Some studies have found that the methodology adopted by Karnataka, in Nali Kali, has contributed to reduced dropout rates and increased enrolment, retention and attendance in the schools. There is a reduced burden of textbooks, homework and tuitions. Some studies have revealed that children reportedly enjoy learning in Nali Kali schools, and their self-confidence and responsibility levels have risen. They have become more independent and feel a sense of freedom. They learn without help and rarely need assistance. A higher level of motivation and a positive sense of achievement in learning were also found. Some studies have also noted improved health and nutrition of children in these schools.

The principles on which Nali Kali is based are sound and have stood the test of time. Nali Kali has endured and has now gone way beyond the DPEP experience in Karnataka in the mid-1990s. Heralded as one of Karnataka's 'most successful, innovative and revolutionary' pedagogic reform programmes, it has flourished in the state. Over time, it has expanded and benefitted other states: Tamil Nadu, Rajasthan, Madhya Pradesh, Assam, Jharkhand, Maharashtra and Chhattisgarh.

The fundamental principles of Nali Kali form an integral part of the National Curriculum Framework (NCF), 2005. Later, the essential principles also reflected in the Right to Education Act.

Recently, a senior educationist and administrator visited several primary schools in Karnataka, and wrote: 'In December last year, I went to Karnataka as part of a Joint Review Mission for Sarva Shiksha Abhiyan. I visited government schools in Mysore and Chamrajanagar districts where I found the stamp of the work done by Anita years ago. Everywhere I went, the Education Department officials recalled what she had done. I saw schools with strong and involved school management committees, committed school principals and teachers brimming with pride, children from poor and disadvantaged homes learning at their own pace with the Nali Kali materials, clean toilets, and tasty mid-day meals.'

Anita passed away before she could read this glowing testament to the efficacy and enduring nature of the project she nurtured with massive effort a quarter of a century ago.

After Nali Kali, she went on to do bigger things on a larger canvas and attained greater heights. There were two important threads that tied her career together: the first was her unshakeable faith that governance had to be about transforming people's lives, particularly the most vulnerable ones. The second was her desire to challenge, through policymaking and governance, power relations at multiple levels and push for change that ushered in real social integration.

She had firm belief in the ability of the ordinary people to bring about momentous change in their lives.

Her defence of RTE's most contentious provision—the admission of at least 25 per cent children from disadvantaged groups to private schools—represented her values and approach. In a document that formed the basis of the RTE's defence before the Supreme Court, Anita wrote '. . . the [25 per cent rule] is not merely to provide avenues of quality education to the poor and disadvantaged children. The larger objective is to provide a common place where children sit, eat and live together for at least eight years of their lives across caste, class and gender divides in order to narrow down such divisions in our society.'

Anita never received any award or recognition for her work. To her, it was the lives she touched that truly mattered.

Rohan came back to the present and looked around the packed room through glazed eyes, in time to hear the English translation of a tribute someone was paying to his mother in Kannada at her prayer meeting—someone he did not know or recognize.

'. . . She took her work seriously without taking herself seriously. She was a great believer in people. We all had access to her—teachers, students, parents, activists, villagers. She always found time for us. Often when the going was tough, and amidst non-believers, Anita went to the field. The mantra she had devised for herself over the years seemed to work for her: "When you are in doubt, when you are apprehensive about initiating change, go to the schools and spend time with the teachers and the children. Then all your doubts will melt away." And when she came to my school, she would sit down with the children and ask them to sing and dance—to show her the learning ladder and where they thought they had reached. When she came, there was so much promise in the air . . . She held us together with affectionate support—and we worked our hearts off—even though we were fully aware that the painstaking work by people like us would be lost to the world, especially if it was work by ordinary government functionaries and the much-maligned primary school teachers . . . Anita also knew full well that the relentless effort she herself was making would, in all probability, go unnoticed except by those for whom it was intended—the children. And that was her sole reward—and it was sufficient.'

Then there was complete silence—as if every person who heard these words was in complete agreement with every single word they had just heard. The speaker, a primary school teacher who had worked with Anita two decades ago, had travelled over 1,000 miles to pay her last respects.

As Sanjay and Rohan stood together with folded hands to thank all those who had come for the prayer meeting, Rohan saw a motley crowd: family, friends, seniors, batchmates, juniors, colleagues, activists, politicians, creative people, policymakers, educationists, district and block education officers, parents, volunteers, primary school teachers and ordinary people who cared for Anita Kaul. After all, she had always drawn her inspiration from ordinary people. She had genuinely believed that they could take their destinies in their own hands and push for change.

Towards that end, she believed that the National Literacy Movement, Nali Kali, and the RTE were but a few of many paths. There were many more.

Coda

In the Department of School Education, Anita handled the flagship Sarva Shiksha Abhiyan (SSA). The passage of RTE entailed the re-conceptualization of the SSA from the perspective of child rights, especially to ensure age-appropriate admission for out-of-school children belonging to disadvantaged groups, such as scheduled castes, scheduled tribes, minorities, children with special needs and migrants.

Anita also served as Secretary, National Council of Education Research and Training (NCERT), where she led efforts in the process of social deliberation for the National Curriculum Framework (NCF), 2005, to set out what should be taught to the children in India and to recontextualize child-centred theories of learning.

A large part of Anita's work throughout her career was centred on empowering women.

During her tenure in the Department of School Education, she helped strengthen the Mahila Samakhya—a programme structured to enhance self-esteem and self-confidence—to enable women to make informed choices in areas like education and employment. It recognized that empowerment was the most critical precondition for the participation of girls in the educational process.

As Director, Women and Child Development, Karnataka, and Director General of three training institutes, including the State Institute of Rural Development, Anita conceptualized and implemented training programmes that were large-scale, participatory and satellite-based—giving priority to principles of inclusiveness and equal opportunity.

She superannuated as Secretary, Department of Justice, Government of India. She facilitated the passage of the National Judicial Appointments Commission Bill (NJAC), 2014. The NJAC was enacted to bring about transparency in the appointment and transfer of judges to the higher judiciary in India.

Following her retirement from the Indian Administrative Service, she joined the Council for Social Development as its Director. She was supposed to have joined the Centre for Equity Studies in New Delhi, but passed away a week before in October 2016.

IV

Death in Police Custody

When the winds drop and the tide turns
courage and conviction give wind to the sails . .

'HSEB zindabad! Zindabad! Haryana Police murdabad! Murdabad!'

The air in Mahendragarh—a sleepy town in the back of beyond—was filled with the chants of 'Long live HSEB!' and 'Down with the Police!', interspersed with 'Kill the murderers!'.

The poor and backward subdivision in Haryana shares its borders and agro-climatic conditions with Rajasthan. Far from the seat of power at Chandigarh, the state headquarters, a posting to the subdivision was held over the employees of all departments as a punishment. Consequently, the staff in most of the offices was either inefficient or unacceptable to the powers that be for various reasons.

Traditionally, Mahendragarh had had a Subdivisional Magistrate (SDM)—a young entrant to the Indian

Administrative Service. Most SDMs were from outside the state. They had no political links and were duly forgotten after they were posted. The summer Nikita joined Mahendragarh as the new SDM, the town was reeling under exceptionally high temperatures. In her early twenties, she was an outsider to the cadre and the first civil servant in her family. On receiving her posting orders, she had no idea where she was headed. She bought the map of Haryana to locate her destination before the journey. The late 1980s were not quite the years of Google Baba!

The 'SDM House' was quaint and had a massive compound. The place looked old and a little spooky. It was situated outside the small town, flanked by mustard fields. The nearest building was a dingy-looking police station a few kilometres down the road.

The gate to the SDM House was opened by a rather grim looking man with one eye made of glass. 'I am Hanuman, the chowkidar. I have worked for eight SDMs before you,' he said.

Neelam, Nikita's mother, had come along with her to settle her daughter in. She took a look at the place and thought, 'My little daughter will find this a difficult place to work in.'

'Do you think you will be safe here, Nikki? You do have other options, you know . . . Are you sure this is what you want?' Neelam asked, wishing Nikita had accepted the Rhodes Scholarship she had been offered the year she had cleared the Union Public Service Commission (UPSC) examination.

Nikita, on the other hand, was very clear in her mind about what she wanted to do in life—quaint towns in the middle of nowhere, and scary old houses, notwithstanding. She was excited about her first job and was raring to go.

A month later, Nikita returned from a visit to Bassai, the furthest village of the subdivision, in her rickety official jeep. The scorching summer sun was unrelenting. The outside temperatures had touched 45° C at noon. By the time she reached home, she had a terrible headache and was running a fever. Her temperature rose to a 102° C around 9: 00 p.m. She decided to take a Paracetamol and call it a day.

Late that night Nikita was rudely woken up by the sharp sound of the telephone bell. By the time she climbed out of bed and walked up to the landline in the corridor, the phone had stopped ringing. Those were the days of stationary phones and trunk calls. She looked at her watch. It was 11.30 p.m.

'Who could that be? And at this time of the night?' she wondered.

The telephone system in Mahendragarh, like most things, was a decade behind the rest of the world. There were 100-odd phones in the town serviced by a manual telephone exchange. Any number you wanted could not be dialled directly. You had to pick up the handset and request the telephone operator at the other end to connect you to it. This also meant that the sweet voice that answered the phone and said, 'Number please?' knew exactly who had called whom and for how long they had spoken.

'The operator would know who called me,' Nikita mused, as she picked up the phone to find out who had tried to call her at 11.30 p.m.

'Hello, SDM Madam. Who can I connect you to?' said the voice at the other end.

'My phone rang a few minutes ago. Who was it, please?'

'That was the SHO from the thana, madam. Do you want me to call him for you?'

Nikita looked at her watch again. It was almost 11.45 p.m. 'Why did the Station House Officer of the local police station try calling me in the middle of the night?' she thought.

Mahendra Yadav, the SHO of the police station near her house, had accompanied the Deputy Superintendent of Police (DSP) at Mahendragarh when he had come to call on her formally. Sarban Singh, the rather rotund DSP, looked straightforward and a little laid-back to her. Mahendra Yadav, on the other hand, was smarter than his senior—maybe too smart. There was a wily air about the tall and self-assured SHO.

'It must be something urgent. I should call back to find out . . .'

Nikita's stream of thoughts was cut short by the telephone operator.

'Madam, a call for you from the police station again. DSP Sahib would like to speak to you.'

'Jai Hind, madam,' said Sarban Singh.

'Jai Hind. What are you doing at the police station at this time of the night?' she asked. 'Is everything all right?' She heard some noise in the background at the other end of the phone.

'All is well, madam. All is well.' The noise in the background increased. 'No, Madam—all is not well . . . We need help. Right now.'

Nikita heard a sense of urgency in the DSPs voice. Then there was some static as someone took the phone from the DSP's hand. 'Madam, you may need to come to the police station,' she heard Mahender Yadav, the SHO, say in a more controlled voice.

'What's happened? What is that noise in the background?'

'Nothing, madam. Just some agitated criminals. They were complaining about the dinner that the langri—the cook—served at the thana this evening. They have started shouting slogans against the police, madam. I called DSP Sahib to sort out the matter. He was talking to the crowd when—'

'Crowd? What crowd? How can there be a crowd of people in the lock-up at the police station? It's too small and can barely hold six!' Nikita interrupted him.

'Not in the lock-up, Madam—they are in the courtyard of the thana. All sixty-one.'

'Sixty-one? How do you have *sixty-one* people in the thana? And why was I not informed?'

'Madam, these are the electricity wallahs. We had orders from above—all the way from Chandigarh—to pick up all the Union leaders of the HSEB, the Haryana State Electricity Board.'

'I know the electricity board has been on strike for almost a fortnight now. The Deputy Commissioner held a meeting about the issue. But I've heard nothing about detaining the leaders of the HSEB,' said Nikita. She thought to herself. 'Orders all the way from Chandigarh? That's one way to stop further queries—for such orders are sacrosanct, I guess. But why was I not told?'

'They are rogues, madam. Shouting and screaming against the government. Even as DSP Sahib was talking to them, one of them fainted and the—'

'Is he okay—the man who fainted?' she cut him short.

'I don't know, madam. The crowd just went mad. They tried to beat us up! We ran into my office. We have locked ourselves in my office—DSP Sahib, two constables and I. The other constables ran away. Thankfully, the door to my office has double locks.'

As he was speaking, Nikita could hear loud banging on a door in the background. She couldn't understand what was being said, but the voices sounded loud and angry. The DSP must have snatched the phone from the SHO, for she heard him gasp rather anxiously at the other end. 'They are going to break the door down—any time now, madam! A man is dead. Please come fast. Help us—they will kill us!'

The panic in his voice made Nikita rush. She wore a salwar-kurta quickly with a long, thick cotton dupatta. Her head was throbbing and she gulped down another Paracetamol. There was no time to wait for Ghanashyam, the driver, to arrive. She called Hanuman and asked him to bring the keys to the jeep and to open the main gate. As she drove out herself, she told Hanuman to wake up the driver and to call the Senior Medical Officer (SMO), the senior-most doctor in the subdivision.

'Tell them both to reach the thana as soon as possible.'

The thana was just down the road from her house, and right across the newly built Civil Hospital. The main gate of the hospital led to a large square where the ambulance was parked. The Emergency and the OPD were on the left side.

The morgue and a room to conduct post-mortems was on the right, closer to the rear boundary wall.

The police station, on the other hand, was an old decrepit structure with thick walls and high ceilings built several decades ago. The main entrance was a twelve-feet-high arched iron gate, which led into a narrow corridor. The SHO's room was on the right and three office rooms were on the left. Beyond the corridor was a large *aangan*—an enclosed courtyard. A few cells were built at a height of three feet above the courtyard. They bordered the aangan on two sides. There was an L-shaped veranda outside the cells. The remaining two sides of the courtyard had a sheer twenty-feet high wall, with broken glass edges at the top to prevent any entry or escape.

Nikita arrived at the police station at 12.05 a.m. The main iron gate was open. There were loud noises coming from within. 'The constables must have escaped from this gate,' she guessed as she entered. 'I am surprised that the sixty-one HSEB men in police custody haven't escaped through it. In fact, it's quite a mystery.'

She heard loud shouts of 'HSEB Zindabad! [Long live the HSEB!],' and 'Haryana Police Murdabad! [Down with the Haryana Police!] They are murderers!'

'Ah! That is why,' she realized. 'They didn't escape because they are rallying around for their collective cause. None of them thought of escaping from the police station alone to go home.'

There was pandemonium inside. The crowd was too agitated to notice Nikita enter. She stood by the gate and tried to gauge the situation. A group of angry men had gathered outside the room with a large sign in red saying, 'SHO Mahendragarh'. The men were banging on the door and trying to push it open. In the courtyard beyond the corridor, a larger group was milling around. A man was lying on the raised veranda outside one of the cells. Several other men were gathered around him. By the time they became aware of the diminutive figure in their midst, Ghanashyam, her jeep driver, had run inside along with Hanuman—the chowkidar (watchman).

'SDM Madam, SDM Madam! Make way!' Ghanashyam said to the world at large.

And the crowd obeyed, for Ghanashyam, better known as Pundit ji to all and sundry in the subdivision, had a way about him. People tended to obey him. Pundit ji was an institution in his own right. All the detainees apparently belonged to nearby villages. They might not have known the new SDM, but they all knew Pundit ji. Unlike Hanuman, Pundit ji rarely showed off the number of SDMs he had worked with. Yet, it was rumoured that he had seen more than fifteen young men and women come and go over the years.

The commotion stopped and the crowd made way for Nikita. They followed her into the courtyard peacefully. They were very angry with the SHO and his men, but wanted a solution. One of the men, possibly their leader, came forward and introduced himself as Ram Niwas, a Junior Engineer with the HSEB. He led Nikita to the raised veranda where a man lay flat on the ground.

'Look, SDM Madam. They poisoned our man. The police have killed Ramesh!'

The man's arms and legs were sprawled on the ground. His large bulging eyes were wide open. There was some goop trickling from the left side of his lips. Ramesh Chand was indeed dead.

'What happened? When did this happen?' Nikita asked, alarmed.

'He complained of pain about an hour after the *langri* served dinner. I called the SHO, who said it was nothing— only gas. Ramesh tried walking a little to ease the gas. But he soon fell down in immense pain. He died a little after 11.00 p.m., madam,' Ram Niwas replied.

Nikita thought to herself. 'At 11.00 p.m.? And at about 11.45 the SHO said, ". . . one of them fainted" to me, over the phone. Obviously, the man was dead before they called me and they knew it. But they lied. The matter had gone out of hand. They would not have informed me had they been able to hush it up.'

'Madam, he was poisoned!' someone from the crowd shouted.

'They put poison in our food. The police have poisoned Ramesh!' said another.

'Haryana Police, Murdabad! Murdabad!' the crowd chanted.

'My stomach is aching too,' said a man at the back.

'Look, someone is vomiting,' said a man, pointing to a boy retching his guts out in the corner of the courtyard.

'Our dinner was poisoned. We are all going to die!' a man shouted in panic.

'I, too, am feeling sick . . .' said a person standing at the back. He turned pale and shuffled before Nikita's eyes. Some men rushed to catch him before he fell down.

The policemen, who had locked themselves in the SHOs room, were soon forgotten.

'Look, madam, they have poisoned us—the SHO and his men!' said Ram Niwas, once the fainted man had revived.

'We will teach this SHO a lesson!' someone from the crowd shouted.

Seeing the anger on their faces, Nikita did not doubt that if the SHO or his men came before them at that instant, the crowd would lynch them. She realized that the policemen were not safe. Their presence would aggravate the situation into something very nasty. She diverted the attention of the crowd to the welfare of their colleagues.

'Let's talk about that later. First, let us tend to those who are feeling unwell. We need to save them. I need your help,' she said. 'Pundit ji, please go to the hospital across the road. Get a stretcher and someone to help lift the man who fainted just now, and also another for the one who is vomiting. Wait. I will explain what you need to do.' She moved away from the crowd to where her trusted driver was standing and whispered, 'On your way out, take the SHO and his men out of the thana. I am concerned for their safety. These men are very angry and outnumber the police. They can turn violent at any time. After that, go to the hospital and then proceed to the village of the deceased. Go meet his family. See if there is someone supportive there.' Then she turned to face the crowd and asked the leader of the group, 'Ram Niwas ji, to which village does the deceased belong? Pundit ji will first see that someone comes to attend to the sick from the hospital. He will then to go to Ramesh's village in my jeep and bring the next of kin.'

'I know the dead man, madam. Ramesh is from Kanina. His village is only 18 kilometres on the other side of the railway line. I will do what you say, madam,' said Pundit ji with new-found respect for his new boss—someone he had earlier thought of as a 'chit of a girl'.

As the driver left, all the HSEB employees gathered around the SDM. She stood patiently, listening to their woes. There was a fervent debate regarding Pundit ji's journey to Kanina to fetch the dead man's next of kin.

'Ramesh only has three daughters. None of them are married,' said a voice from the crowd.

'How will the girls come at night?' said another. 'Who will light the pyre?'

'Even Ramesh's brother is no more. Maybe his brother's son will perform the last rites,' said a friend of the deceased.

'The SDM did well to send for his family,' Nikita heard Ram Niwas say, as she moved towards the man who had fainted earlier and still looked a little pale. Even before she could reach the spot, she heard another person groan with pain.

'Hanuman!' Nikita called out to the chowkidar, who stood in the corridor. 'Didn't you tell the SMO to come to the thana? Please go and check why the doctor hasn't come yet.'

Before Hanuman could do her bidding, Dr Aneja, the Senior Medical Officer, walked in along with a junior and two ward boys carrying an empty stretcher. He started examining the man who had fainted. His junior went off to examine the man who had vomited and the other one who was groaning with pain.

Dr Aneja called the SDM aside and conveyed his diagnosis. 'There's nothing serious. He is feeling some discomfort, but there is nothing wrong with him physically. Looks more likely anxiety. He'll be fine.'

'Why don't you send him across to the hospital and keep him under observation?' said Nikita.

'But, madam, I think it is only psychosomatic,' the SMO opined.

'I think so too. The ones I examined show nothing worrisome either. It's possibly psychosomatic,' added the younger doctor.

'That may be so, Doctor Sa'ab but please let them stay in a hospital bed for the night. Make them feel more comfortable.' Then, looking at the angry faces around her, she added, 'Yes, take them to the hospital. Give them the best treatment.'

The crowd around her softened. Some even smiled at their new SDM.

Even before the stretcher with the man who had fainted, left for the hospital, there were others who started to complain of pain in the stomach. Nikita urged the doctors to examine all of them. Within half an hour, seven HSEB employees in police custody were sent to the hospital across the road. There seemed to be an epidemic of sorts at the thana.

'What do I do with them, madam? There's nothing the matter. In fact, *you* need to rest. You appear to have a fever,' Dr Aneja said to Nikita, as the last patient left.

'I'll be fine. Just make the men comfortable. Give them some vitamins. Maybe a saline drip will help,' she answered, as she walked the doctor to the main gate.

The corridor was empty. The policemen seemed to have been be forgotten by the crowd in their effort to assist their peers. Nikita walked into the now empty office of the SHO. Ram Niwas and another HSEB leader followed her into the office. Before the two men could react, she turned from the door to talk to them. 'The police wallahs have apparently gone. They must have slipped away, while we were trying to attend to the sick. Doesn't matter. I am here with you all. I will be here until this matter is sorted out. I will get to the bottom of why and how Ramesh died in police custody. The others, who are falling sick, need to be taken care of.'

'Ramesh Chand is a hero of the HSEB cause,' said Ram Niwas. 'The SHO is not to be trusted. The guilty must be punished. We have full faith in you, madam. We know you will do us justice.'

'We can't thank you enough, SDM Sahiba. You have saved the lives of so many!' said the man accompanying him.

'Please don't fold your hands. It's my duty. I just need to make a call to the Deputy Commissioner at the district headquarters to inform him about this incident.'

She saw Ram Niwas and his companion about to leave the room, and asked them to wait while she made the call. She offered them a chair, unsure of what would happen when they were told the others about the policemen having left the premises. 'You don't need to go. Please sit down, while I wait for the call to the DC to go through. Hanuman will make us some tea. Help me understand this. Why were so many of you locked up in the thana?'

Ram Niwas started talking animatedly about the demands of the Electricity Board Employees Union, about how they had gone on a 'pen-down strike' initially; how the full-fledged strike that ensued later was declared illegal by the government under the Essential Services Maintenance Act (ESMA). Apparently, a decision had recently been taken at the Police Headquarters in Chandigarh that all the Union leaders of the HSEB should be apprehended as a precautionary measure. The Superintendent of Police of Mahendragarh district had called her deputies for a meeting. She had told them to round up the leaders and all the important people responsible for the strike. The identity of the 'important people' to be caught was nebulous. The DSP had asked the SHOs to prepare a list of all the residents of their circle, who had gone on strike. The SHO Mahendragarh, in his wisdom, had decided to pick up every man in his jurisdiction, who was an employee of the HSEB. He was quite pleased with himself at his achievement. And that was how sixty-one HSEB employees were housed in the courtyard of Mahendragarh thana that evening.

'The administration was not informed, Ram Niwas ji. I had no idea,' said Nikita. She thought to herself as the phone rang, 'And I don't think I would have ever been told about this had Ramesh Chand not died in police custody, and had the sixty other men detained in the thana not turned against the SHO.'

The telephone operator informed Nikita that DC Narnaul was at the other end. He was a stern-looking man. Nikita had met him just once after joining duty as the SDM. She looked at her watch rather nervously. It was 2.45 a.m.—hardly the time to call a boss, leave alone one who was rather strict. 'Good evening—er—good morning, sir.

Sorry to disturb you at this time, but something urgent has come up . . .'

As soon as she finished briefing the DC about the evening's events, she heard him say: 'I am leaving Narnaul in a bit and will reach Mahendragarh as soon as I can.'

'Sir.'

'I am ordering you to conduct a formal "inquest" immediately. You will receive the formal papers later. Please start right away.'

'Yes, sir. Right, sir,' said Nikita, feeling apprehensive. She thought frantically, 'An inquest? Good lord! What in God's name is an inquest? And how on earth do I conduct one when I don't even know what it means?'

Nikita could hardly let on that she had no clue about what the DC had directed her to do. She had no desire to ask him to explain what he meant by an inquest. There was no one to turn to.

'Can you help me?' Nikita asked Ram Niwas. 'Please call Dr Aneja, the SMO, on the phone and tell him that the DC has ordered an inquest. Ask him to come to the thana. The DC is on his way from Narnaul. And, can your friend please go to the aangan and see that no one touches the dead body? I will go and get some papers I need.'

Nikita hurried out of the room in search of solitude. She left Ram Niwas feeling rather important as he picked up the phone to call the SMO. She walked across the corridor into the first room she saw. The record room of the police station was filled with metallic racks stacked up with dusty files. She closed the door and leaned her aching head against the cool metal of the file rack.

'Inquest, inquest, inquest . . . now where have I heard that word before?'

Nikita shut her eyes and searched her memory. Suddenly, her mind went back to a misty morning in Mussoorie. The clouds were coming in through the open window of the lecture hall at the Lal Bahadur Shastri National Academy of Administration. She breathed in the scent of the pines. As she looked out of the window, Nikita envisioned wild daisies atop the hill beyond. The booming voice of Professor D. Bannerjee echoed in the background. Dada Bannerjee, as he was called by the probationers, was a favourite Law teacher. He taught so well that any class he took was literally dinned into their heads.

'Inquest! Nikita, come back from the clouds! What is an inquest? When is an inquest ordered? Under what Section? What steps will you take to conduct an inquest into the cause of the death of a person? Come, tell us. Let me begin for you . . . An inquest is to be conducted under Section 176 of the Criminal Procedure Code. Now—step one: you will first . . .'

Every word Dada had said in class that day came tumbling back to her— every single word—in his loud voice, laced with a strong Bengali accent. He had ended the session with: 'In so many years that I have taught probationers at the Academy, I have heard of only a few young IAS officers who have had to use this section. In all probability, you will never need to conduct an inquest in your career. But who knows? You could be one of the rare ones. So, know the procedure and learn all the essential steps.'

'Thank you, Dada. Bless you,' Nikita sighed.

She sent up a small prayer thanking D Bannerjee, from the record room of a thana, on that sultry night, while her fever continued unabated despite the Paracetamol. She marched into the courtyard, confident that she knew exactly what she had to do. The SMO had arrived, along with a photographer who was taking photographs of the dead body from different angles. He had also brought the requisite papers and handed them to Nikita. She was back in command.

'Have you called a team of doctors to conduct the post-mortem?' she asked Dr Aneja. 'I know they can start only after sunrise. But it's almost 4.00 a.m., and the sun will rise soon. They should be at the hospital latest by 5.30 a.m.'

'I have done so, madam' said Dr Aneja. And then, in a softer voice, he shared his opinion with the SDM. 'The post-mortem will reveal the cause without a doubt but, to me, it looks like a heart attack—especially after I got the medical history from the deceased's nephew, Sanjay. Your driver brought him to the hospital and I have brought him here to the thana with me.'

Nikita looked up to see Sanjay, the dead man's nephew, standing at the back of the courtyard with the HSEB employees—watching her examine his uncle's dead body.

'Knowing what to do from Dada Bannerjee's class in the sanitized environs of a classroom, and thoroughly examining a dead body at a police station, are quite different things,' she reflected.

The men in the courtyard surrounded her, and watched her every move from a distance. She proceeded with her examination of the dead body to see if there was anything untoward, including any fresh injury marks.

'And am I supposed to touch this solidified goop dribbling out of his mouth?' she wondered.

Around 4.30 a.m., the DC arrived from Narnaul, along with the Superintendent of Police of the district. He addressed the crowd of the HSEB employees standing in silence at the other end of the courtyard. He assured them that a fair and transparent inquiry was being done, and said that they should have faith in the administration.

'We have full faith in our SDM, sir. But the police must be punished. They have poisoned us.'

'Ramesh Chand is dead. So many are in the hospital. They, too, would have died if SDM madam had not come on time.'

'Yes DC Sahib, SDM madam saved their lives,' a chorus went up from the crowd.

There was a hint of a smile on the DC's face as he turned to Nikita. When she escorted him out of the police station to his car, he told her that he was leaving the thana but would be staying at the guest house. He asked her to be careful. 'This crowd is okay as long as they trust you, as they do now. But they are restless, and seething with rage under the surface. Anything can spark a violent reaction.'

'I will be, sir,' Nikita replied, thankful that the Deputy Commissioner and the SP were staying the night in the town. It was heartening to know that in case something went wrong, she had someone to turn to barely a kilometre away.

'To me this looks like the lull before the storm. Things will get worse once the news spreads and union-wallahs from other districts come down in the morning.'

Nikita nodded. She hadn't thought of that.

'We could have a violent riot on our hands. The SP has requisitioned more force, including armed constabulary from

Rewari. He and I will camp at the Mahendragarh Guest House until this trouble blows over. Please stay calm and collected,' said the DC.

'Yes, sir.' Nikita knew there was a great deal of truth in what he had said.

'I am leaving the DSP and my gunman behind for your protection.' Then he actually smiled as he looked up, and said, 'Apparently, you don't really need them, Nikita. These people seem to treat you like a bit of a hero.'

'No, sir . . . yes, sir. I have contacted the deceased's family. His nephew is here and he's very supportive. I've also ordered the post-mortem to be done at the earliest,' she mumbled, recalling how much at sea she had felt a little while earlier.

'Good. Get the post-mortem done as soon as you can after sunrise, and hand the dead body to the relatives for cremation at the earliest. His body is a potential cause for statewide unrest. Please call me in case anything untoward happens at any time of the night—or morning,' he said, looking up at the sky. It was almost dawn.

Nikita finished the physical examination of the dead body quickly, and started filling up the documents. She told Dr Aneja to transport the body to the hospital for the post-mortem. After sending the body to the morgue, she left for the hospital to visit the men who had been admitted. Through the night a few others had complained of physical discomfort and had been escorted there.

By morning, there were thirteen HSEB employees at the same hospital. The centre of action shifted from the thana to the Civil Hospital by 5.35 a.m. Pundit ji parked the SDM's jeep next to the ambulance, opposite the 'Emergency' inside the main gate. Nikita got off the jeep and entered the hospital. Some of the HSEB men were already inside, attending to the sick. The others, who were either roaming around or sitting in small circles in the square, followed the SDM into the ward. They stayed at a distance, watching her, as she went from one bed to another along with the doctor, to ask after the welfare of their comrades. During the rounds, Dr Aneja informed her that the doctors for the post-mortem had arrived and had started the procedure.

By the time Nikita came out into the open quadrangle within the hospital premises, it was 6.30 a.m. The sun was up and the HSEB men were idling in the quadrangle where the SDM's official jeep was parked. She looked at the small mortuary at a considerable distance behind her, and hoped that the post-mortem would be over soon.

She picked up the megaphone that always lay at the back of her jeep but had never been used before. Now, for the first time, she spoke to the HSEB employees through it. She told them that the men in the hospital were being looked after, and were fine, as they had seen for themselves. She said that they could go home if they liked since the doctors were looking after them. 'You don't need to wait for the post-mortem. The report will, inter alia, form a part of my inquest report and reveal the cause of the death. Once we establish the cause—and if there is even an iota of doubt—please believe that I shall personally ensure action is taken against the guilty.'

'We trust you, madam. But we will wait for the doctors' report,' replied Ram Niwas.

The men nodded in affirmation, and sat down on the ground in a circle.

A little after 7.00 a.m. Dr Aneja came out and announced the preliminary findings, which confirmed his own suspicions the night before. 'The team of doctors has found that the cause of death was a heart attack. There is no occasion to suspect food poisoning. Still, we will send the viscera to the forensic laboratory at Madhuban for testing today. As I talk to you, the doctors conducting the post-mortem are stitching up the dead body. It will be handed over to the family soon.'

Nikita asked Sanjay, the nephew of the deceased, to speak over the megaphone next. He thanked the doctors and the SDM. He informed the group that his uncle had been a diabetic as well as a heart patient.

'We will take his dead body to our village, Kanina. The cremation will be held later this morning. You all are welcome to add a log of wood to the pyre. We—'

Before Sanjay could finish his sentence, loud shouts were heard from the road outside.

'HSEB Union, Zindabad! Haryana Police, Murdabad!' An angry mob of 200-odd employees from the neighbouring district marched in, shouting slogans loudly. The silent-and-peaceful crowd sitting inside also stood up and started shouting with them. The sloganeering continued for a while.

From the corner of her eye, Nikita saw the DSP slip out and hide behind the ambulance, which was to double up as a hearse. It was now parked outside the mortuary, waiting to take Ramesh's body to his village for cremation once the post-mortem was over.

The SDM was left facing the crowd alone. She allowed the men to shout for a while to vent their angst. Then, once again, she picked up the megaphone and started talking to the crowd, urging them to sit down. She could see the newcomers being told to obey by the others.

'She's the SDM—and she's on *our* side. She saved our men. Listen to her,' she heard someone say.

Nikita asked the doctor, and then Sanjay, to repeat their speeches. As time elapsed, and the morning advanced, she realized that more and more unions from other districts would also arrive and the crowd would swell. She called the DC's gunman and told him to go to the guest house and inform her seniors that she could soon need police assistance from outside the subdivision.

Her fears proved right. In a little while, she could hear the chants of 'zindabad-murdabad' coming from both directions of the road. The peaceful crowd inside stood up again to welcome their compatriots from the neighbouring towns and districts, and echoed the 'zindabad-murdabad' raucously.

Once again, Nikita waited patiently for the fervour to die down before she picked up the megaphone to speak to the crowd. She was beginning to feel weak, and her voice was hoarse with all the shouting. She handed the instrument over to Dr Aneja. She glanced at her watch and looked at the mortuary. It was already 9.30 a.m.

'If the post-mortem is over, why haven't they handed over the dead body to the family yet?' she wondered nervously. 'Go check what's wrong,' she whispered to Pundit ji.

Her driver came back to tell her something startling. 'They are waiting for a sheet to cover the dead body.'

'What! So where is the sheet?' she asked anxiously.

'There is no sheet, madam. The nurse in charge of the stores refuses to give one until she has a written order from the doctor.' Pundit ji refrained from telling Nikita that the nurse had said, 'How will I account for a lost sheet? I am not going to pay for any shortfall out of my salary. The post-mortem bodies are wrapped in shrouds brought by the family, not in hospital sheets.'

Nikita was appalled. With every passing moment, the problem was escalating.

Dr Aneja spoke to the crowds, and told them about the findings of the post-mortem, for the third time that morning. Nikita rushed to the morgue with Pundit ji in tow, and into the room where the post-mortem of Ramesh Chand's body had been conducted earlier that morning. The doctors, who were sitting in the ante room, tried to stop her and then followed her into the room.

On a table at the centre of the room lay the loosely stitched naked body of the deceased, Ramesh Chand, awaiting a shroud. The memory of the body with organs poking out of gaping holes stayed with Nikita for a long time. But this was no time to think of anything but the problem at hand. She quickly took off her long and thick khadi dupatta and handed it over to the junior doctor.

'Cover the body with this. Quick! And then place it in the ambulance, please.'

The urgency in her voice had the right effect. She headed towards the square to follow the ambulance. Her official jeep with a sign saying 'SDM' in bold, was parked at a fair distance from the crowd. She heard Sanjay over the megaphone, yet another time, making his request to allow the body to be cremated. As she reached the square to climb into her jeep, a truck stopped outside the main gate. A new group of loud and angry men entered the hospital gate, chanting a new slogan: '*Hamara* hero Ramesh Chand *amar rahe, amar rahe!* [Long live our hero, Ramesh Chand!]' along with the usual, 'HSEB, Zindabad! Haryana Police, Murdabad!'

By then the crowd sitting inside the hospital premises had swelled to about 800 people.

Nikita picked up her megaphone and gave an impassioned speech. 'You all know that Ramesh Chand was not poisoned. The doctors have conducted a post-mortem, and Dr Aneja has told you several times that he died because of a heart attack. Even Sanjay, Ramesh's nephew, says that . . . Ramesh's wife and daughters are waiting in Kanina to cremate the dead body. The ambulance is carrying him to Kanina . . . Please do not disrespect your friend's body. It will rot if it lies unprotected in this heat any longer. I am going to pay my respects. You should also come for the cremation.'

Nikita saw Ram Niwas speaking animatedly to a bespectacled man who had just arrived in the truck.

'Ram Niwas ji, I want to speak to you and your leader separately,' she said.

The bespectacled man walked up to her authoritatively, and said: 'Ramesh Chand is our hero!'

'Yes!' repeated the crowd. 'Ramesh Chand is our hero!'

'We will not allow his heroic body to be sullied and taken away in the vehicle of a government that does not care for, or hear, the voices of its own employees. The HSEB Union will take him in their own truck and cremate him with fanfare. Our truck is parked outside the gate.'

The truck they had hired was too big to enter the main gate of the hospital. Nikita was alarmed. They could take the hired truck with the dead body anywhere as that of a martyr and a symbol of their cause—across the state to Chandigarh, to the Boat Club in Delhi . . . anywhere! She was aware that a dead body had a strong emotive appeal, but she did not argue.

'Okay, so at least let the ambulance take the body to the gate. And Sanjay must accompany the body of his uncle too. He is to perform the last rites,' she offered.

'That's all right.'

The leaders started discussing amongst themselves about who would sit in the truck and accompany the HSEB martyr.

Nikita walked across to the ambulance and seated Sanjay and Pundit ji inside. She told Pundit ji to sit in the driver's seat and to take the ambulance straight to Kanina. Then, she took the keys to the SDM's jeep, and whispered, 'The truck is on the left side outside the hospital gate, Pundit ji. Turn to the right and drive fast once you are out. Cross the railway line on the road to Kanina. I'll drive the jeep and meet you there.'

The HSEB employees were jubilant that Ramesh Chand, their martyr, would be carried in their own vehicle. They started pouring out of the main gate. Nikita drove her jeep slowly behind the ambulance carrying the dead body. As they exited the gate, the ambulance revved up and sped off to the right, while the crowd was moving towards the truck parked on the left. The SDM's jeep whizzed past them before they could understand what had happened.

As she turned round the corner, Nikita saw the armed constabulary from Rewari, the neighbouring subdivision, march into the hospital premises—led by a DSP. She drove at breakneck speed and crossed the railway line. The railway crossing was a manned one.

Pundit ji said to the person manning it. 'Now close the gates. And keep them shut.'

Nikita sent the ambulance to the dead man's village, and stood beside her jeep at the crossing. Five minutes later, a truck stopped on the other side. Ram Niwas, and the man she had spoken to earlier, along with a few angry men, had followed her jeep frantically. They got off the truck and stood across the shut gates.

'I am sorry, but I cannot allow you to disrespect the dead body of your colleague. Nor will I permit you to cause any trouble in a subdivision where I am in charge of law and order. The post-mortem has been done and I have started an inquest. The body of Ramesh Chand is on its way to Kanina where his family is waiting to cremate it.' She took a deep breath as she looked in the direction of the village where Pundit ji had driven the ambulance with the dead body. 'I am going to Kanina to offer my respects, and to convey my condolences to the family. It will be nice if you all reach the cremation ground, too, and offer a log of wood to build the pyre as a mark of respect.' She folded her hands in a solemn namaste and drove off without a backward glance.

Violence that would have swept through the district, and across the state, by the employees of the HSEB Union on strike who were set to declare the dead man as a martyr to their cause, was averted without the use of a single bullet, or a tear-gas shell or even a lathi.

Coda

Ramesh Chand was cremated at Kanina at 12.00 p.m. The SDM walked to the cremation ground with bare feet—as per the custom—on blistering sand to attend Ramesh Chand's cremation, against the local custom. Traditionally, girls did not go to cremation grounds in the region.

Senior leaders of the HSEB Union also reached in time to pay their respects. The angry crowd, which might have turned violent had the dead body of their 'martyr' remained on the spot, withered away—without any use of force.

The SDM returned to Mahendragarh in the afternoon and went to report the turn of events to the DC and the SP at the guest house. The Divisional Commissioner had reached there by then, and was pleased about the manner in which the matter had been handled. The DC said, 'It's not us, sir. The hero of the day is this young SDM.'

The forensic report arrived five days later and confirmed the findings of the post-mortem. There was no poison in the viscera of the deceased. The SDM's inquest report stated the findings that Ramesh Chand had died a natural death.

A week later, the government of Haryana negotiated a settlement with the employees of the State Electricity Board. The strike was called off. Ramesh Chand, 'the martyr' of the two month long HSEB strike, was forgotten.

Nikita proposed that the eldest daughter of the deceased should be given a government job. Until a regular job was provided by the Electricity Department, she appointed Ramesh Chand's daughter at a temporary post in her office.

She also wrote to Professor Banerjee, thanking him for his brilliant lecture which had proved to be very useful.

Ten years later, Nikita was posted as the Deputy Commissioner of a district neighbouring Mahendragarh. Her reputation preceded her as: 'The SDM who courageously faced a crowd of 10,000 men in Mahendragarh.' In people's minds, the 1,000-strong angry crowd agitating against the custodial death had somehow swelled into a bloodthirsty mob of 10,000 men! Nikita had a long and meaningful career in the IAS and she continued to work with commitment, conviction and courage.

V

Development Despite Red Violence

Violent red over dismal poverty
compassion and courage is all it takes . . .

Dr Malini V. Shankar, the Chief Executive Officer (CEO) of the Zila Parishad of Chandrapur, was startled by a knock on her door around 8.00 p.m. She was on an inspection tour to Jiwati, the last village of the district on the Andhra border. Jiwati was situated in Rajura taluk, amidst a thick forest where you couldn't see humanity for miles. On her way back, as the sun went down and it grew darker, Malini decided to stay the night at Gadchandur. The sudden knock on the guest-house door startled her. A strange sound in the Naxalite belt was enough to alarm anybody after dark.

'Who is it?' she asked nervously.

'The police! Please open the door.'

Malini peeped through the keyhole. She saw that a posse of policemen was indeed standing outside the door.

116

'Or could it be the Naxalites dressed up in police uniforms?' she thought.

All the stories of encounters Malini had heard about since she had joined as the CEO of the Zila Parishad or the District Council of Chandrapur in 1988, played in her mind.

'Which police? Where are you from . . . which thana?'

'There's been an ambush—it is urgent we talk to you, madam.'

'But I don't know you. We will speak in the morning.'

'Bobde here, madam. A contingent from the Maharashtra Police is standing here with me. They want to speak to you. Please open the door. Something terrible has happened.'

Malini recognized the voice of her faithful driver, Milind Bobde. She peeped through the keyhole to make sure that it was really him before she unlatched the door. Bobde walked in with an inspector. Six other men stood just outside the door, crowding the entrance.

'Madam, the jeep carrying your escort party was ambushed on its way to Gadchandur. They tried to return the fire, but were outnumbered by the Naxalites. Five of the six men died before we reached the spot. We found only one man still breathing. We have brought him here to the healthcare centre, but he is not in a good state. He may not even last the night. Could you please record his "dying declaration"?'

Malini was shell-shocked. She remembered how, after she had finished inspecting the primary health centre at Jiwati, Bobde had told her that he 'did not feel comfortable' and that they should leave for Gadchandur earlier than scheduled. The escort party was having their tea and some snacks. Malini had told them to finish their tea and to follow her jeep as soon as possible—not later than twenty minutes.

In the last one year since her posting, Malini had learnt to take security warnings seriously. Her security was a matter of concern due to the large presence of Maoists. Chandrapur was a Naxalite-prone area, and it was prudent to follow security protocol. On the other hand, in order to build a rapport with the people to ensure development in the area, it was imperative for her to talk to the villagers and the tribals without the presence of her security personnel. Malini found that the presence of security staff tended to intimidate the local people and distance them from the administration. She had learned to maintain a fine balance. Each time she left Chandrapur town on tour, she would travel in a different vehicle with the security officers following her after a time lag of about twenty minutes—so as to allow her time alone with the local inhabitants.

So, when she had told her security people to follow her after twenty minutes, as Bobde drove her out of Jiwati, she had merely followed her normal protocol. And now, five young men had been killed in cold blood.

Malini was shocked by what the policemen told her. She was pained at the loss, but shook her head in refusal as she turned to them. 'I am sorry; it is not possible for me to do so. I am not an Executive Magistrate. Not all IAS officers in the field are. The District Magistrate (DM) and the Sub-Divisional Magistrate can, for they are given the requisite magisterial powers. My role as the CEO, Zila Parishad, of the district, is a developmental post as against a regulatory one.'

As the police were about to turn away, she stopped them. 'Wait. Give me your wireless handset. I will call the SP, and the DM, and ask them to send an EM to record the man's dying declaration right away. We are only three-and-a-half hours away from Chandrapur.'

Once the police left, Bobde turned to the CEO and said, 'Madam, we should leave early tomorrow morning.'

Malini went to the health centre to see if they could move the injured man to a larger hospital in town. Later, she found that the man was Amol Mohite. He had recently returned from leave after visiting his wife and newborn daughter—his first child. She was told by the doctor on duty that Amol was critical. There was no way he could be shifted to the hospital in Chandrapur. He would not survive the journey.

Malini did not sleep a wink that night. She looked up at the stark sixty-watt bulb and the cobwebs at the corner of the ceiling, and her thoughts went back to her father, a Visiting Scientist at the US Air Force Base. His last letter was full of concern about her safety. He could never quite understand what his brilliant daughter was doing travelling in the forests of Maharashtra—making herself a sitting duck to the violent Naxalites who didn't think twice before killing anyone in a government vehicle.

Dr Malini V Shankar had been surrounded by books from the day she was born into a scholarly middle-class family in Madras: law books that belonged to her grandfather—a barrister at law; her mother's books on Sanskrit literature, and books on every subject under the sun read by her father—a scientist. As a result, Malini continued to study for years on end—for the love of reading, and to gain knowledge for the sake of knowledge. A bachelor's degree in chemistry was followed by a master's in forensic science, and a master's in chemistry from Massachusetts. Thereafter, she enrolled at the Ohio State University for a PhD in organic chemistry. The scholarship came close to the salary of an Assistant Professor. One day, Malini took a leave of absence from her doctorate to appear for the All-India Civil Services examination. Later in life, she also picked up a public policy PhD in institutional economics from the Indian Institute of Technology at Chennai (IIT-M); a management degree from the Asian Institute of Management, Manila; and a diploma in international economics from France.

The civil services examination had opened up new doors for her to an entirely different life from the academia, and brought her to Chandrapur.

'While pondering over rings and chains of carbon, hydrogen and oxygen in Ohio, who would have ever thought I would be lying sleepless in the back-of-beyond—grieving the loss of five short lives, worrying about a wounded man hovering between life and death, and wondering whether the next bullet or landmine would be meant for me . . .' Malini thought to herself. She stayed awake, staring at the ceiling on that horrific night in the rest house in Gadchandur.

The next morning, she was driven to Chandrapur by Bobde just as the sun was rising. On the way, she stopped at the health centre to see how Amol was doing and to try to shift him to the district hospital, if possible. The doctor told her it was quite impossible, and it was now only a matter of time.

'A matter of time before another life is snuffed out for no reason; a matter of time before a young woman is widowed, and a child orphaned before she is a month old!' Malini was angry at the senseless violence and the unfairness of it all.

Had there ever been the slightest doubt in her mind about whether or not she had made the correct choice in joining the IAS, as against a less stressful career in the academia, the events of the previous evening wiped it out completely. She was convinced that she was here in Chandrapur district for a purpose: to help in the development process and to ease the lives of those who were caught between poverty and violence.

The name Chandrapur means 'Village of the Moon'. The city lies at the confluence of the Zarpat and the Irai rivers. The latter has a history of flooding. Chandrapur is also known as the 'black gold city' due to the vast reserves of coal in the Wardha Valley Coalfield and in other parts of the district. Located about 150 kilometres south of Nagpur, the district borders Adilabad district in present-day Telangana. Chandrapur city is the headquarter of the district by the same name in the remote Vidarbha region of Maharashtra.

There are many Stone-Age sites in the district. In 322 BC, Hindu and Buddhist kings ruled Chandrapur until it was annexed by the British in the 1850s. Initially a part of the vast Mauryan Empire, over the years Chandrapur has been ruled by the Shungas, the Satavahanas, the Vakatakas, the Rashtrakutas, the Chalukyas, and Seuna or Yadava dynasty. In 9 AD the Gonds—Adivasi tribals—took it over. The Marathas conquered it in 1751 and ruled for 100 years. The last Maratha King died heirless, and Chandrapur was taken over by the British. They called the district Chanda—a name that was later changed back to the original name of Chandrapur.

Until 1981, Chandrapur was the largest district in India with a dense forest cover and abundant wildlife. Now there are some engineering factories, and also a few super thermal power plants due to the availability of coal in the region. Besides coal, the district has vast reserves of limestone—raw materials for the local cement industry. Chandrapur is known for its forest cover and wildlife. Abundance of bamboo, wood and *sabai* grass in the area was the basis for the setting up of the Ballarpur Paper Mill in 1956. The forest cover notwithstanding, there was a great deal of pollution from the coal and limestone mines as well as the paper and cement factories.

Despite the rich natural resources, the people were poor and the infrastructure weak. Chandrapur was one of the least developed districts in Maharashtra. There were no all-weather roads. Communication was weak. The poor lived in abject poverty and under extreme violence. The Maoists had found a good breeding ground amongst the impoverished tribals. They managed to establish a rapport with them and convinced them that they were acting in their interest —those who had 'not been given their due'. The Naxals embodied a response to sociopolitical and economic inequities with slogans like, 'Liberation against State Repression.' The district was called 'Kaalapaani' in the administrative circles—one from which no one returned unscathed.

Naxalites with Maoist leanings from the neighbouring Adilabad, in Andhra Pradesh, extorted money from industrialists in Chandrapur and terrorized the villagers. In the 1980s, they had started to carve out a guerrilla zone in the underdeveloped tribal areas of eastern Maharashtra. Gadchiroli, once a part of Chandrapur district, became the red bastion in the state. Along with Gondiya, Yavatmal, Bhandara and Nanded districts, it was declared as a 'Naxal-prone area'. The Maoists had around 250 full-time armed cadres and a strong contingent of about 3,000 local supporters. Police records reveal that more than 80 per cent of the people killed in exchanges between the police and the Naxalites, were the tribals.

Against this backdrop, Malini had joined service. Around the time she joined, the elected body had been dissolved. Hence, she was also made the Administrator of the District Council of Chandrapur besides being incharge as the CEO-ZP. A month after she started working, the Secretary, Rural Development, Maharashtra, came to visit the district from Mumbai. He was aghast to find her posted there.

'Which idiot posted you here?'

She calmly responded, 'The government, sir.'

'Well, the government must make amends then,' he said with a laugh. 'You—a young girl from Tamil Nadu—all on your own in Kaalapaani. That's not fair. And why did you not protest when they posted you here?'

To his surprise, Malini said, 'I am happy to be posted here, sir.'

'Let me get back to Bombay. We will transfer you immediately to an area that is not so tough.'

'No, sir, please do not,' Malini pleaded.

'But why? Anyone else would jump at the offer.'

'Chandrapur has remained backward for too long. A great deal needs to be done here and, in the last one month, I have come to understand the place and the people. I want to work here, sir. I *like* working here. Please do not transfer me out. I would like to be able to make a difference to the lives of the people. I know I can make that difference.'

The Secretary looked at her earnest face and sighed. 'Well then, you have to call my office every day at 4.00 p.m. to let me know you are alive and kicking. And if I am away on tour, or busy in a meeting, please leave a message with my secretary.'

Malini was touched by her senior colleague's concern. His directions were rather difficult to comply with. She tried for a week and then stopped, after promising that she would not do anything foolish and would always take the security guards provided to her each time she went on a tour outside the city.

Initially, after her promotion, Malini had been reluctant to take the job of the CEO of the Zila Parishad—not so much due to the area she was posted in, as to the nature of the work. Having played only regulatory roles after joining the service, she was apprehensive since she had not worked in a developmental job. The responsibilities of the CEO-ZP were onerous, spanning a wide spectrum: health, education, social welfare, tribal welfare, roads, irrigation and specific interventions for the welfare of women and children.

She took a liking to Chandrapur the day she set foot in the district, while she stared at the frog in her room in the Circuit House. Her work soon made her realize her penchant for development activities. She enjoyed every moment of the assignment, for it gave her great satisfaction. She gave it her best, though she was exposed to a range of issues: industrial unrest, forest and tribal conflicts, the after-effects of mining, unemployment, and underdevelopment besides, of course, the overarching Naxalite issues.

One of the first things that struck Malini during her first few weeks in the district was that the Naxalites' presence had brought development to a non-existent level in the major portion of the region. They collected money and terrorized the villagers as well as the officials on the ground. Extortion from private companies—the paper industry in particular—that needed bamboo from the forests for manufacturing paper—was the order of the day. In the name of revolution, using the slogan, 'People's War for People's Government', the Naxalites were mobilizing the local people.

Government funds meant for tribal and rural development often remained unspent. At the end of the financial year, they were returned to the exchequer as 'unspent balance'. The amount 'spent' for development was sometimes siphoned off or fell into wrong hands.

In the absence of the elected members from both the Zila Parishad and the Panchayat Samiti, it was incumbent upon Malini to tour the place as frequently and as widely as possible. She covered every tehsil and block at least once a month. Since the Naxalite movement was widespread in the late 1980s, the government had issued strict instructions for the officers to undertake travel only after intimating the DM. They were also to be accompanied by an escort vehicle with a posse of policemen holding sten guns.

'How can I implement and monitor development projects with a bunch of armed men accompanying me wherever I go?' Malini wondered.

'Well, that is a standing instruction. It is essential for your safety, and to prevent any mishap. You cannot travel without the escort vehicle,' the DM had said to her.

Given the constraining instructions regarding the tours, Malini strategized her visits such that they were both effective and safe. She opted to leave her official car at the premises of the Sub-Divisional Officer and used the jeep of the Agriculture Officer or the Social Welfare Officer—the two officers that were viewed by the Naxalites as non-exploitative. She would take the police escort provided to her, but request them to keep some distance. She could then accomplish her task in a freer environment without their presence antagonizing or intimidating the villagers and tribals.

And here she was, on her way back from the remote Naxal-affected Jiwati on the border of Adilabad, after her visit to the primary health centre located on a hilltop, mourning the loss of the men who had been tasked with her safety. She, too, would have been dead but for her driver Bobde's suggestion that they should leave earlier than planned.

'If only the men in the escort vehicle had finished their tea earlier . . . If only I had insisted that they stop eating right away and follow our jeep. If only . . .' Malini was upset.

'Madam, there is no answer to the "if onlys" of the world. There is no way you could have stopped what happened. When Death comes, who can say "nay" . . .? Who knows what lies beyond this turn?' Bobde replied in the matter-of-fact manner of one who had seen a great deal of tragedy and continued to live on the edge.

'Yes, but they were all so young. What did they do to deserve this?'

In the districts, the driver and the personal assistants are an officer's confidantes, and also a repository of memories. Malini had learnt to respect Bobde and his rustic common sense.

'Madam, what do we all do to deserve what life brings us? Our cards are dealt when we are born. It's the finesse with which we play our hand that determines how we journey in this world.' There was much wisdom in his words. 'We, in Chandrapur, are like frogs in a well. There is nowhere else we can go. So, we fight poverty and the Naxalites fight us. You officers come and go. We remain where we were.'

'Yes, that's true, Bobde,' Malini replied. She recalled that he had seen nine CEO-ZPs come and go.

'I, too, will possibly go like Amol and the other men some day . . . But I like driving you around, madam. You go to places no one has been to before. You even go to far-flung villages, meet our people . . . You talk to them and spend the money that comes for them on them.'

'Bobde, I merely do my job. I do what I have to.'

'Madam, that is what is commendable. Most officers sit in their offices, scared of these terrible Naxalites. They while away their time until they are posted out of Chandrapur. You don't know it, but you are a rarity.'

'Don't embarrass me, Bobde. The people of Chandrapur deserve much more.'

'No, madam. Let me say this. We all remember the incident about the threat written in blood—and how it did not deter you from doing your duty. We always will.'

Bobde's words brought back the memory of an incident two months earlier. Late one night, Malini had returned from an official tour. She noticed a stranger pacing back and forth in front of her house. She thought it rather odd for the late hour, and rushed indoors to call the SP. He told her not to worry, and assured her that the man pacing outside her door was a policeman in plain clothes whom he had assigned on the beat. It was said that the police had intercepted a letter warning Malini of dire consequences if she went on with her ways, purportedly written in blood!

'I have just finished posting out schoolteachers. It is perhaps a disgruntled teacher resisting his transfer in this novel manner,' Malini had laughed.

The threat to her life written 'in blood' did not stop her from going through with the posting orders. Nor did it deter her from travelling to the far-flung and underdeveloped regions of Chandrapur. She continued working undisturbed, and earned the reputation of a committed intrepid officer who meant business.

Malini learnt about sickle cell anaemia first-hand. For the first time in her life, she saw for herself the terrible stunted growth amongst children, and its harmful effect on adolescents and adults. Sickle cell anaemia was prevalent amongst the tribal population. Malini started an awareness campaign about the disease in the predominantly tribal areas of the district in a mission mode. The Gonds in the three Naxalite-affected tehsils spoke a native tongue which was a mix of Marathi, Telugu and Tamil. Her own mother tongue, Tamil, a working knowledge of Marathi, and a perfunctory knowledge of Telugu, helped her in gaining the trust of the community. The initial faith went a long way in generating awareness and preventing the infection with vaccination, high fluid intake and folic acid supplements.

Malini ensured that the medical facilities were built, and maintained, by the ZP even in the remotest areas, so that they were geared up for treatment. She followed up with the CMO to ensure that there were sufficient provisions of the requisite antibiotics, painkillers, hydroxycarbamide or hydroxyurea. People who needed blood transfusions, and a small percentage who could be cured only by a bone marrow cell transplant, were not turned away for the lack of facilities.

The traditional set of officers who thought in silos wondered what Malini was up to.

'What does a CEO-ZP have to do with health? What is this campaign against sickle-cell anaemia?' said an officer who had been posted in Chandrapur for a year, and continued to lament his luck throughout the year.

'The Health Department should be taking care of such things, Malini; it is really none of your business. Except for setting up medical facilities and maintaining them, what role does a CEO-ZP have in healthcare?' opined a colleague.

'Actually, in a perfect world, I wouldn't have to . . . but how can I not do what I can when I see such painful effects of a malady, which can easily be averted by simple precautionary measures? Besides, I am there only because the people who need to do their job are not doing it—and I am merely filling in a void.'

The quality of education was another important area where Malini had a marginal role to play as the CEO-ZP. She made small but important interventions that made a difference. On one of her tours to inspect new classrooms being constructed by the ZP, she was amazed to see children, supposedly, reading lessons from books held upside down in their hands.

Disturbed by the poor standards, Malini took it upon herself to inspect the schools across the district personally. In due course, she discovered that the problem revolved around the teachers. In some of the far-flung villages, they did not attend school. Some merely came on pay day to receive their salaries. The ones who did attend lacked both knowledge and basic teaching skills, having been recruited for reasons other than merit.

Malini put the block education officers on notice. She transferred some of the teachers who were habitual absentees but, having worked in the same school for decades, had developed a strong local nexus. There was much heartburn. They had strong political backing, and were a force to be reckoned with, as their local 'guardian'—a minister—was the president of the teachers' union.

Malini decided against suspending the teachers, as it would be an infructuous and counterproductive step. Instead, she focused on improving their basic knowledge and teaching skills. She initiated summer camps. Even the teachers' unions appreciated the exercise. For a young officer with no roots in the state, she received massive support when the minister acknowledged the efficacy of the camps, in a public speech, attended by over 1,000 schoolteachers. Malini forged ahead with her efforts in improving the delivery of education in Chandrapur.

There was no more talk of the quality of healthcare, or education, or an enhanced tree cover in the district being 'strictly none of your business'.

The government had launched an exercise to recruit teachers locally for the Zila Parishad primary and middle schools. The interview committee at the district level interviewed more than 250 potential candidates. Their qualifications ranged from class ten-pass to a master's degree. Malini was disappointed to observe poor knowledge and weak application of the mind in most candidates. Many got even the basic directions wrong and showed the sun rising from the west. Malini was pleasantly surprised to interview a candidate who had recently finished class ten and came from a very remote area. He knew the provisions of the Constitution and its interpretation, was adept at mathematics, and was even familiar with the works of the Marathi litterateurs.

'The headmaster of our school, Mr Gajanan Narayanrao Murkute, is very inspiring, madam. He has built a small library, which subscribes a newspaper in our remote village in Rajoura taluka. Even though the newspaper reaches us after two or three days, it is an important part of our school curriculum. Every morning, before school hours, he calls us home and has us read a part of a book beyond our curriculum, as well as a newspaper article. Every child is required to share an item from the news in their own words during the assembly. During the last period, he gathers the whole school, picks up a topic, usually current affairs and authors, and discusses it.'

'That is amazing!' Malini exclaimed.

Mr Gajanan Narayanrao Murkute became an important strategic partner in Malini's efforts in improving the basic knowledge, teaching skills and pedagogic techniques in Chandrapur. Gajanan was the person who warned her about rampant cheating in the board exams, and told her about the 'supply chain' in the copying industry!

In early 1989, the local tabloids were replete with reports of mass copying by the schoolchildren in the state board examinations, and of an administration that turned a blind eye. Malini took it upon herself to stop, or at least curtail, the rampant cheating in the exams. She had some authority over the ZP schools. She learnt that every year, the state government in the Education Department issued an order authorizing officers to inspect the examination halls. In the era of snail-mail, the order invariably reached the districts late—often on the last day of the examinations. She dispatched a team to Mumbai to obtain the orders by hand. She then ensured the issuing of detailed executive orders authorizing the teams to inspect the exam centres, making them responsible for ensuring fair examinations. The exams were Malini's first ringside view of vested interests at work.

At an examination centre she went to inspect herself as a part of the random checking, the gates were locked from inside to prevent outsiders from entering. Initially, the policeman posted outside refused to permit her to enter the examination hall, even after she showed him her authorization letter. Malini had to get his superiors to read out the rules to him. By the time she got the gates to the exam hall opened, she saw scraps of paper being thrown out of the windows like *phuljharis* or crackers. Several jute bags full of shredded paper were picked up as evidence. At another centre, some boys ran away from the exam hall as soon as they spotted her vehicle. A young girl had hidden booklets to help her cheat in the pleats of her sari. The inspections were a real eye-opener.

'No wonder the people I interviewed for the position of a schoolteacher could not point out that the sun rises from the east—leave alone being able to do simple sums involving fractions and percentages,' she thought to herself.

During the investigation, Malini discovered a rather structured and institutionalized 'supply chain' that connected the examinees, the invigilators, the owners of government-aided schools, and even the board of examination. In order to stop the malpractice, she had to understand the procedure involved. This supply chain was strongest for the English and the mathematics exams. She requested the Collector to shut down the Xerox shops on the days when the exams of these two subjects were conducted.

Having undertaken the task of ensuring that copying and cheating were not permitted in the 1989 Board exams, she diligently submitted a detailed report to the government. Nothing ever came of it. A few months later, to her astonishment, she received a letter from above, asking her as the CEO-ZP to explain why the pass percentage in the district of Chandrapur had fallen as compared to previous years. The letter went on to state that the low percentage of examinees who had passed the mathematics examination was a matter of concern. She was required to explain why the level of education had been declining in the district despite the summer camps for the teachers she had recently begun.

'You should not feel bad, dear. Just carry on the good work. You will always receive some flak while making a change,' Malini's father had said in his last letter. The letter had revealed the philosopher in her scientist father. 'You can sit by the edge of a pond without making a ripple all your life. Or you can choose to jump into the cool waters, and swim across to the green meadow on the other side. Now *that* will surely cause many ripples.'

She folded her father's letter and put it inside the envelope neatly. Then she looked across at the other one lying on the table—the one she had received from Mumbai, asking her to explain the poor performance of the school students in Chandrapur, and directing her to take corrective measures. The missive had completely ignored the report she had sent earlier, regarding rampant cheating and actions that needed to be taken against the nexus that perpetuated it. She decided to ignore the communication. Instead, she started preparing for a new capacity-building programme for schoolteachers, and continued to tour the region for developmental work.

'One good thing is that trees are planted wherever I go,' she thought.

Malini sometimes went a few kilometres on foot to visit project sites, much to the pleasure of the tribals. She found that her frequent tours had a collateral advantage for the environment. Sharing her tour programme with her workforce often meant that the tree cover along the route would improve. Anticipating that she would also inspect the plantations along the way, as she drove through the countryside to a school, a panchayat ghar or a health centre, the withered saplings along the route she took were invariably replaced. Each time she travelled, the actual tree cover on ground increased.

In the course of her tenure, she worked with committed officers, enlightened union leaders, empathetic villagers and supportive colleagues and seniors. The Finance Minister, who was touring the area, once said to her, 'I am sorry the government had to post you here. Somebody had to go. Most of our local officers manage to stop their posting to Chandrapur through their links. An outsider to the state like you becomes an easier choice. I hope you don't mind.'

Without hesitation Malini told him that she was very happy. 'I truly love my work. I would like to continue here as long as I can,' she said, and she meant it. Her work gave her immense satisfaction. Every effort produced a result that made a difference to the lives of many who were without succour.

'I am glad to see young officers enthusiastic about working in the most challenging regions.'

The two years in Chandrapur passed away too soon. If only time did not have wings! When she left Chandrapur to return to Mumbai, many organizations and people paid rich accolades to the committed CEO-ZP, as they bade farewell to her.

Malini's most rewarding moment was when a tribal village invited her to inaugurate the start of the sowing season. She had introduced soya bean cultivation to the farmers the previous year. Following an abundant harvest, they had made good money. One village requested her to sow the first seeds of the new season on the day she handed over the charge. The plough was fitted with a cup into which she had to gradually insert the seeds to be ploughed in the soil. Clad in a sari, Malini stood on the plough driven by a pair of bullocks. What a memorable moment it was!

As she left Chandrapur, the plantation of soya bean became an accepted practice. Malini left behind a legacy in more ways than one, and in several fields: health, education, employment, agriculture, income generation, infrastructure and forest cover, in addition to her mandated role as CEO-Zila Parishad.

Coda

Dr Malini V. Shankar is presently the Vice-Chancellor of Chennai-based Indian Maritime University, under the aegis of the Ministry of Shipping. Her initial years spent in remote areas reinforced her interest in building human capital.

She was also the Chairperson of the National Shipping Board—the top advisory agency to the government on shipping-related matters. She held the post of Director General of Shipping, and was responsible for maritime administration, in the country until she superannuated in December 2018.

Malini worked mostly in three sectors: water, industries, and shipping. Her noteworthy contributions have been in the water sector, including the Maharashtra Sujal Nirmal Abhiyan, the Integrated River Basin Plan for the Godavari Basin, and the E-jal Seva computer information system.

Her most challenging post in Maharashtra continues to be CEO-Zila Parishad, Chandrapur, followed by Principal Secretary (PS), Water Supply and Sanitation, and PS, Irrigation—a post held by engineers for four decades until Malini joined the department. She firmly believes that her accomplishments are the fruits of the good wishes of the people she has served.

VI

Sand in the Eyes

*I face the sun and walk right on oblivious to
the dust on my feet and the sand in my eyes . . .*

'Go slow! Don't face the wind. You'll get sand in your eyes.'

Durga Shakti ignored her mother's warning. She shook her head and laughed as she ran barefoot on the beach in Goa. The sand tickled her toes. The sea breeze caught her hair. The spirited five-year-old ran ahead with her hair flying behind her, and she laughed louder—ignoring the sand in her eyes.

Twenty years later her mother's words came back to her in a flash. Greater Noida's new Sub-Divisional Magistrate (SDM) shook her head, as if to push the image away. Having lived in a city all her life, the memory of that beautiful day brought a smile to her face. It is strange how some images and words stay untouched in your mind for years. Then, suddenly, they come to the fore at the strangest of times in the strangest of places.

Durga Shakti had a peculiar affinity with sand. The soft white sand on the beach was all she remembered of the family holiday in Goa when she was a child. The sand on the banks of River Yamuna, flowing through her home town, was darker and heavier. She was born in Agra and had spent her childhood there. She loved playing on the riverbanks. Her father would often take her down to the Yamuna opposite the Taj Mahal. She would pile the damp sand over her feet, and squeal with joy as her father helped her build castles with it.

Durga Shakti's father was a civil servant. He had sweated in the sweltering heat and dust of Agra while dealing with encroachments upon government lands, especially in the vicinity of the river Yamuna. He was always bubbling with energy. Durga Shakti had often heard him say, 'Things on ground zero are far different from what we hear or find in the files.'

Durga Shakti belonged to a middle-class family. Her parents liked powerful names for their children. So their daughter, though small and petite, was christened Durga Shakti after the mighty Goddess. A name, they hoped, would inspire her through life—for Goddess Durga was never quite afraid of anyone. And a name, they thought, would protect her as well—for Goddess Durga brought fear into the hearts of the wrongdoers.

Durga Shakti sighed as she remembered the number of times she had been teased about her name at school. Even one of the members of the UPSC Board, taking her interview, wanted her to talk about the source of her name, and find out whether she knew other appellations.

Twenty years after her introduction to sand in Goa, Durga Shakti looked around at the dark room and sighed again. This was no time to dwell upon fond memories of the carefree days she had spent with her family. She had to act. She shook the memory off. But her mother's words on that sunny morning echoed in her mind. 'Go slow! Don't face the wind. You'll get the sand in your eyes.'

Should she do just that? Keep the sand out of her eyes? It was definitely an easier option. She blinked as she remembered the threats, and tried to take a decision. 'Should I take the goons head on? Or should I look the other way and let things be? Wouldn't it be easier to allow things to go on as they have done for years before I arrived in Greater Noida?'

She remembered how thrilled her father had been when she was selected for the Indian Administrative Service. He had sat her down to tell her how blessed she was. Then, taking her hands in his own, her father had said something that stayed with her. 'And now you must contribute to the public good without fear or favour.'

Durga Shakti was assigned the Uttar Pradesh (UP) cadre. After completing her training at the LBS National Academy of Administration at Mussoorie, she had been posted as the SDM of Greater Noida in September 2012. Greater Noida, a part of Gautam Budh Nagar district, was a relatively new city on the outskirts of New Delhi. It was a place of pride for Uttar Pradesh. It had sprung up almost overnight in the midst of a largely rural habitation. By the time Durga Shakti took charge of her first posting, it had a fairly good infrastructure and excellent connectivity to New Delhi. The city was growing at a rapid pace. Farming was receding towards the floodplains of the Yamuna. The dangers of rapid urbanization to the environment were being flagged, both by the experts and by the government authorities. The expressway and its proximity to Delhi were the major drivers of growth. It was primarily fuelled by realtors, investors and the construction industry.

Around 2012, Greater Noida was a city of the future. There was sufficient space. The development of real estate, high-rise residential towers, elite villas, commercial areas, educational institutions, healthcare facilities, and recreational and sports avenues were at various stages. Despite rapid construction, major parts of the city looked desolate. Most of the residential complexes had been bought by investors and remained unoccupied. The extensive infrastructure of this new and planned city was still awaiting its residents. There were vast vacant tracts of barren land, just waiting to be built into an urban forest.

When Durga Shakti took charge as a Magistrate, the crime rate was high. Gruesome murders and robberies were common in the city's largely unguarded spread and on its wide empty roads. Criminal gangs were not uncommon.

Since construction was the order of the day, sand was a precious commodity. Sand was readily available on the banks of the Yamuna, which flowed close to Greater Noida. Its illegal dredging was encouraged by the extensive demand from the construction industry. Unlawful mining was a flourishing business for the sand mafia.

One balmy October evening, a fortnight after she had joined the very first job in her life, Durga Shakti was driving along the Delhi-Noida-Delhi Expressway. Ever since she had joined office, she had been touring the area frequently to see the conditions for herself, and to understand the lay of the land. After all, like her father said, 'Things on ground zero are far different from what we hear or find in the files.'

The vast stretches of agricultural land on both sides of the expressway were lush green. It had been a long day. The fragrance of the rice fields and the cool breeze lulled Durga Shakti into a gentle slumber.

'Madam! See!'

Durga Shakti heard the words, as if from afar. She opened her eyes to see her driver, Ram Lal, pointing to an overloaded lorry being driven rather rashly ahead of them. The lorry driver was driving at a crazy speed, probably having fun on the largely empty expressway.

During training, Durga Shakti had been told that anything and everything in her subdivision was her job. She decided to stop the truck and check it. Ram Lal blew the siren, drove faster and waved the truck down. The lorry driver, barely out of his teens, stopped the truck. Then, without much ado, he jumped off and rushed towards the fields. Durga Shakti was nonplussed. She had thought she would stop the speeding truck and warn the lorry driver against rash driving. And here she was stuck with a loaded truck, abandoned by its driver in the middle of nowhere.

'He's carrying illegal sand, madam', Ram Lal informed her with the air of someone who knew it all. He belonged to the area and had driven the SDM's vehicle for several years. He had seen many SDMs come and go. 'This truck is not alone. Most likely, it is the "pilot" truck that signals the others that all is clear.' He parked his own vehicle on the side of the road. 'The other trucks normally follow the pilot.'

'Is that so?' asked Durga Shakti, alarmed. 'Ah, something interesting is unfolding,' she thought to herself.

Illegal mining of sand had not been a part of the briefing when she took over the charge of the subdivision. No one had warned her about the sand mafia.

'Now that the pilot has run away, he will warn the others. You won't see them on this stretch tonight for sure, madam,' said Ram Lal.

His words proved true. They waited for almost an hour. No other sand lorries were to be seen. Soon it was dark. Durga Shakti decided to leave after noting the number and make of the abandoned truck. She went back to her office and wrote a preliminary report to enable her to lodge a formal First Information Report (FIR) with the police. Then she picked up the phone and spoke to the Senior Superintendent of Police (SSP) of the district, and urged him to intensify police patrols along the expressway.

There was a long silence at the other end. 'Okay. Let me see,' he said.

The SSP was much senior to her both in age and experience. Durga Shakti had a feeling that the SSP's curt 'okay' was laced with humour. He was probably amused at this late evening call from a new entrant to the local administration, and her suggestions in the vast 'badlands' of the state of UP.

'Sand is just a larger and coarser particle of dust, but it is still just that—dust,' Durga Shakti reasoned with herself when she went to sleep that night.

She had done her bit, she thought, and slept soundly. Before she slept, she decided she would put a stop to this unlawful business in her subdivision. She had no idea what lay in store for her, what the winds would bring her way in the near future. Nor did she realize what she was landing herself in, or how many apple carts she would be upsetting in the process.

And why would anyone want to pay for mere dust? More so when it was readily available free for the illegal miners, and at a cheap rate for the builders? Illegal mining was a win-win situation for all—and the basis of a very strong nexus.

Durga Shakti soon realized that the poor lorry drivers picking up sand to make an extra buck were a mere façade. They represented the face of a rich, well-oiled and protected underground kingdom. And like any underground mafia, these people were powerful—nay—demonic.

Amidst the numerous roles she performed as the SDM, unlawful sand mining and its unchecked trade became a priority for Durga Shakti. Thanks to the young lad, who had abandoned his truck on the highway, she dug deeper into the intricacies of the sand mafia. With Ram Lal as a teacher, she studied their modus operandi to understand how they managed to get away with rampant violations of the Mines and Minerals Act, 1957.

Mining cartels were operating in the region with apparent impunity. Sand mining was widespread. The sand mafia operated mostly at night. By the time daylight broke, trucks laden with sand would secretly disappear from the public eye, having unloaded their cargo at the door of the flourishing construction industry. She learnt that a powerful nexus, with deep pockets, had remained unchecked and held sway over the region for several years. The situation was tough and demanded a conscientious and bold strategy. Obviously, the sand mafia had misconstrued the term 'mine'.

The illegal sand dredging 'industry' was rather hi-tech and well organized. The dredging sites were guarded with armed goons perched at elevated points. More often than not, the sand trucks were escorted by SUVs with men carrying weapons to protect the cargo in the lorry. They possessed sophisticated dredging equipment.

The demand for sand far exceeded the supply. Hence the mining had gathered pace with every passing day. The adverse impact of extensive sand mining was manifold— both economically and ecologically. It had caused massive destruction: of crops, contributing to the river changing its course, and endangering floodplains and depleting the ground water table. Besides the brute exploitation of a valuable natural resource, illegal mining of sand had also led to a massive economic loss to the exchequer in terms of loss of royalty.

As time passed, the nexus had grown stronger and richer. With money had come power and a sense of invincibility. No one had bothered the lawbreakers so far. No one would. That was the general belief. And definitely not a young woman— barely five feet tall!

That evening, when she returned home after her first brush with illegal sand transport, Durga Shakti called her two dependable colleagues—Ram Lal, the driver and Avinash, her committed Personal Assistant. They told her what was, apparently, common knowledge but spoken about only in hushed voices. They named the people who were rumoured to be involved in some way or the other. As she glanced through the list, Durga Shakti realized they were the who's who of the area. All powerful, all well known.

'We must put a stop to this,' she muttered to herself.

But she must have said it aloud, for she heard Ram Lal say, 'To "stop it" is a must. But who will? It's not easy.'

'It's tough, but there's no way I can look the other way,' Durga Shakti thought. Aloud she said, 'Let's see. At least let's try. They are in the wrong. We have the might of the government behind us.'

'When confronted with a difficult situation, every person has a choice to either take responsibility or look the other way.' Her father's words echoed in her mind.

Once she had decided that she would put a stop to the unlawful mining of sand in her subdivision, there was no looking back. The next morning Operation Sandstorm began. The first thing Durga Shakti did was to reach out to senior officers in the district and then the police. She shared her experience, and her decision to stop to the illegal mining, and sought their help. Both the District Magistrate, her immediate boss in the district, and the SSP, were very supportive.

'Great,' said the District Magistrate. 'Go ahead. Just ensure that you plan it properly.'

The SSP was very helpful and assured her that he would provide her with as much police force as she required. Fortified with this support, she felt strengthened and started to plan her next move. After all, an individual backed by the government's might and all its resources could not, and should not, feel helpless—however strong the sand mafia might be!

Durga Shakti felt reassured. Patrolling along the highway was heightened the next day. Soon, random checking of lorries at odd times became a norm. Lorries ferrying illegal sand were stopped and seized. Midnight operations were conducted to chase and check the sand-laden trucks. The SDM's jeep led a caravan of vehicles every day to stop vehicles carrying illegally mined sand. The chase required them to travel at great speeds and sometimes along dirt roads. It was both scary and risky.

Many vehicles engaged in illegal mining were seized in a short span of time. Several miscreants were caught. Many lorry drivers were arrested. Some managed to get away. Sometimes, a driver would dump the sand on the road and race ahead with the empty lorry as soon as he realized that he was being chased. The pile of sand in the middle of the road would slow down the vehicles chasing him, and create a massive roadblock. More often than not, the lorry driver merely jumped out of the lorry and fled, leaving the sand-filled lorry on the road. Vehicles carrying illegal sand were seized. Several FIRs were lodged.

The campaign was fast turning into a pretty spicy tale for the media. There were prominent headlines in the local papers almost on a daily basis. Around this time the UP government, in far-off Lucknow, issued executive orders that directed the administration across the state to come down heavily on the illegal mining mafia.

Armed with the circulars, Durga Shakti decided to up her game. She realized that so far, they had merely caught petty pawns. Despite their best efforts, they had merely touched the tip of the iceberg. The drivers of the sand-filled lorries represented the surface, and were mere employees earning a few rupees. They knew nothing. They had little at stake.

'We have only caught the small fries. After two weeks of constant patrolling, we have been able to build a scare. Yet, we have not been able to make even a tiny dent in the underground network. We catch a driver here and there, but the illegal mining goes on unabated,' Durga Shakti said to her team one evening after a long and arduous chase. 'I think we need to change our strategy. Let us strike at the root. We need to reach the main kingpins.'

The area along the banks, and the dried bed of the Yamuna flowing through the subdivision, was mapped. A reconnaissance report of the illegal mining sites was prepared by two trustworthy field officers. Teams of trusted and courageous civil servants of all ranks and policemen were carefully selected. Raids were planned and executed at the mining sites. The idea was to nip the menace in the bud—at the site itself.

Simultaneous raids were conducted virtually, on a daily basis, at two or more locations along the river. Complete secrecy was maintained. In order to prevent any leakage of information, only Durga Shakti and a trusted colleague knew the exact location they would be raiding. The others in the team would be informed just a few minutes away from the actual spot.

The dredging sites had rings of elevated points used by armed men to guard the mine. The powerful men who ran the illegal operations took full care to protect their operations. Sand mining and dredging was a well-organized business, as well as a regular and easy source of income in the area. The money it generated was unaccounted for and grew exponentially. The illegal miners worked the mines with sophisticated equipment. They had even built makeshift bridges to facilitate the access of machinery and lorries through different sand blocks. The terrain was difficult, and there were deep ravines where previous dredging had exhausted the sand.

Most of the raids were conducted at midnight. The raiding parties had primitive means and equipment. But they were very high on zeal and commitment. They were able to go past the armed guards, dismantle the infrastructure and seize the expensive equipment. This stopped the mining process and actually hurt the organized set up. The persistent raids, and the dismantling of the equipment and infrastructure on the mining sites, pinched the sand mafia where it hurt.

Operation Duststorm proved to be a success. The stealthy attacks on the mining sites proved to be very effective. Illegal mining of sand came to a grinding halt in several parts of the subdivision. Hundreds of people were arrested. The momentum of the concerted raids on the dredging sites, and on the transporting lorries, sent the brazen sand mining mafia into a tizzy.

Greater Noida, being close to the national capital, received greater attention from the media—both print and electronic—than any other subdivision would normally receive in the hinterland or far-flung districts. The movement caught the media's eye and was transformed by them into a corruption-crusade overnight. They went wild with coverage of the action being taken.

Around this time Durga Shakti, the five-feet tall and yet daring SDM of Greater Noida, started getting threats from different quarters through different means. Her family, and seniors in the department and in the district, stood firmly behind her. Her parents had come to stay with her when she was a few days into the crusade against the mafia. The local media and the people supported her. Durga Shakti ignored the threats and went after the sand mafia relentlessly. She felt good about the satisfying work she and her team were doing to rid the region of the menace.

And then the hammer struck and her world came crashing down around her. One evening, tired after a full day's work, she slept earlier than usual. The day before, she had slept only for a couple of hours. She and her team had raided a mining site and the operation had concluded at 2.30 a.m. Durga Shakti was in deep sleep when her phone rang. She was shaken awake, and she saw her uncle's number flashing on the screen. She looked at the time. It was 10.30 p.m.

'How are you, Durga Shakti?' She heard a hesitant note in her uncle's voice.

'What's up, Uncle? Should I get Dad?' she asked.

'No, no it's you I'm worried about,' he said. 'Have you seen the news?'

'No, I slept early. Was out late last night,' Durga Shakti replied, stifling her yawn.

'Switch on the TV. Now.' There was a sense of urgency in his voice.

Durga Shakti reached for the remote. As she turned the television on, she got the first taste of the 'system'. All news channels were constantly flashing 'Breaking News', stating: 'Noida SDM suspended!'

It made no sense. It took a while for the word 'suspended' to register.

'Suspended? How is it possible? And what have I done?' Durga Shakti was clueless.

She had not even completed a year of service. She sat down as waves of deep anguish and helplessness alternated with the feeling of shame. She ran into her parents' room. They tried to comfort her.

'This decision has no legs to stand on'—she heard her father say through a haze.

'But what have I done to deserve this?'

Her fate seemed to hang in the air. She had no idea what lay ahead.

'Your actions against the sand mining mafia must have upset many powerful people. Some of them are rather important, you know. You have deeply hurt the interests of several people who stand to gain from the politics of it directly or indirectly. Most likely that's the reason,' her father said.

'But I did nothing wrong there. They are the ones who are indulging in unlawful activities. So why am I being suspended?'

'This could be the result of a deep conspiracy to dislodge you, Durga.'

'This will tarnish my image as an impartial and upright officer. What do I do?'

Durga Shakti's disappointment turned into despair, and then anger, at the system.

'It's too late to find out. Go to sleep. Tomorrow is another day,' her mother said softly.

Sleep eluded Durga Shakti that night—and her parents too. She could hear their muffled voices in the next room till early the next morning. She could scarcely wait to reach office. Once there, she felt that all the people were staring at her. She held her head high as she walked past them and entered her room. She had no reason to feel ashamed for her actions. If anyone did, it was the lawbreakers—the sand mafia!

There it was, lying on her table—a sole brown envelope deciding her fate, bearing the stamp of the Government of Uttar Pradesh. Her fingers shook as she opened it and read her suspension orders. The body of the order stated that she was being suspended for 'potentially disrupting communal harmony' in the village of Kadalpur.

Durga Shakti looked at the order in amazement. 'Kadalpur? Communal harmony? Good Lord! What is this all about?'

She sat down on her chair, took a deep breath and buzzed the intercom. 'Bring me the yellow file titled "Kadalpur", Avinash,' she said, as her Personal Assistant stepped inside the room. 'I emailed the advance copy of my report from home to the DM the night before last. Did you not send the hard copy to his office yesterday?'

Durga Shakti remembered the telephone call she had received as she was returning home from Kadalpur two days ago. It was from the DM. He wanted her to submit her report on the Kadalpur episode immediately. She had reached home, typed a detailed report immediately and emailed it to the DM within two hours, perplexed at the urgency, but had treated the request as a purely routine matter.

'I did, madam. It went out yesterday. In fact, I checked with the DM's office. They received it the same day too,' Avinash informed her, handing the file over to her.

She opened the file and started to read its contents to try and make some sense. She scrutinized all the relevant papers: the court order, the DM's order, her spot report, and the other documents.

'The encroachment was removed. The action was in compliance with the orders of the Supreme Court. It was done under orders of the DM. It was sorted out peacefully. Just yesterday, a few residents of Kadalpur came to my office to invite me to a nikah (a Muslim wedding) in the village . . .' she reminisced. 'What is happening?'

Kadalpur was a small village in Dankaur block of the Greater Noida subdivision. On a humid Saturday morning, Durga Shakti had been tasked with the responsibility of demolishing an unlawful construction on government land. A 'boundary wall' was being constructed illegally, ostensibly for a new mosque in the village. The Supreme Court of India had passed orders prohibiting the unauthorized construction on government land. As ordered by the District Magistrate, Durga Shakti drove to the venue with a view to comply with the orders of the Court in letter and spirit. The situation demanded extreme restraint to be exercised.

Kadalpur was normally a law-abiding village. Still, she needed to tread with caution. Religious sentiments could easily flare up the situation. More so with a mosque involved in the month of Ramadan. Durga Shakti was rather wary.

Before leaving for the village, she had clearly briefed the team accompanying her. They were to wait for instructions from her. Under no circumstances should their actions inflame antisocial elements.

On arrival, the team spoke to the Panchayat Secretary and the elders of the village. Durga Shakti showed the orders of the Supreme Court, and apprised them that the construction of the boundary wall was in violation of the apex court orders. By this time her reputation as an honest and fair officer had spread in the subdivision. Surprisingly, there were no arguments. Nor was there any resistance from the community. In fact, the people building the wall agreed to bring it down themselves.

The meeting with the villagers was both cordial and peaceful. After the wall had been brought down, Durga Shakti spent time with the people to see the spot where they wanted a new link road to be constructed. Immediately, she directed the Junior Engineer accompanying her to draw up plans for constructing the road, and approved it in principle. The whole village was in a celebratory mood. An all-weather link road was a long-due necessity. Later, they all had walked back to the community hall and shared tea. As a token of their affection, Durga Shakti and her team had been offered dates customarily eaten to end a fast during Ramadan.

'What a happy ending to a potentially inflammable situation.' Or so Durga Shakti had thought then. 'And now this?' Durga Shakti squirmed as she looked down at the ugly words on the paper she held: '. . . hereby suspended, pending an enquiry.'

She picked up the file and drove to the DM's office. She was informed that the DM was in a meeting. She sent in her slip and decided to wait. With every passing minute, the walls seemed to close in.

'You received the orders?' said the DM when he saw the paper in her hand.

She nodded silently.

'These are tough times,' he said. 'You should relax, think logically, and start framing your response to the charges.'

Durga Shakti stared at her feet while the DM talked. She felt helpless as she walked out. Suspended!

That day, Durga Shakti was enraged, and keen to destroy the falsehood of it all. Her parents let her talk the anger out of her system. Tired, she slept that night dreaming of the soft white sands of Goa. The next morning, as the sun rose, it brought an unexpected new ray of hope. The action against Durga Shakti had sparked a massive outcry. The decision of the Government of Uttar Pradesh to suspend her had blown lots of sand and dust. The national outrage that followed was unprecedented. The sudden deluge of support was overwhelming and almost unbelievable.

In the next few days, Durga Shakti's pictures were splashed all over the newspapers and news channels across the nation. Social media was filled with stories about this courageous young SDM and her fight against the sand mafia. The cameras mobbed her wherever she went. Her story was flashed by national news on a daily basis on prime time for almost two months, along with the concomitant endless debates and loud exchanges. The national media presented her as the face of anti-corruption. A national battle for justice seemed to have begun on her behalf.

The aftermath was the real test of the young SDM's perseverance, upbringing and training. It would have been easy for anyone in her twenties to be swayed by all the attention. She could have grabbed the opportunity to make anti-government headlines and 'off-the-record stories'. The media would have lapped it up. They hounded her, waiting anxiously for a single byte from her.

Durga Shakti, however, maintained a dignified silence. She refused to talk to the media and stayed away from the glare. She prepared a detailed response to the charge sheet, defending her actions to the government, meticulously, as per the extant rules. But she never uttered a word against anyone—and never defended herself in public. Throughout the period, which was rather traumatic for her, Durga Shakti shied away from the cameras that hounded her relentlessly, and did not make a single appearance on television. Her calm and fortitude later became the fulcrum around which her conduct was judged.

She received unconditional support—without seeking assistance from anyone. Political leaders, including the then Prime Minister, sympathized with her and spoke up against the wrong done to her. State cadre Indian Administrative Service associations, and the Indian Police Service associations, across the country, issued statements condemning the incident. She received umpteen letters of support from complete strangers. Several public interest litigations were filed in the Allahabad High Court as well as the Supreme Court of

India, by concerned citizens, demanding the quashing of her suspension order. Youths across the country carried out candlelight marches, calling for the revocation of her unfair suspension.

If you Googled the 'most Googled celebrity in India' during August 2013, Durga Shakti's name would come up as the number-one choice.

Perhaps, Greater Noida's proximity to the country's capital was a major reason for the wide attention given to Durga Shakti's cause. She was grateful for the support, and often wondered whether she would have received such huge backing had she been posted in a far-flung subdivision in a remote district. She would have had to fight a losing battle alone.

Despite the national uproar in the media and elsewhere, her trauma persisted for six weeks. Each day presented a new test: of her character, her patience and her tenacity. Even as she put up a brave face in front of her parents, she woke up every morning hoping that it was the last day of her trials.

The pressure on the UP government mounted—against pursuing any disciplinary action—every passing day. The state government realized that perhaps a mistake that needed to be rectified had been committed.

Six weeks after she had received her suspension orders, the government decided to revoke them. The arbitrary charge of 'potentially destroying communal harmony' was withdrawn simultaneously. The charge by the government—and the withdrawal of the charge—were both without any provocation from her side.

One fine morning the headlines in the newspapers, and the news channels, across the country, blared: 'Durga Shakti reinstated with full honours!'

She turned to look at her mother and smiled. 'Look, Ma. The storm is behind me. There was a lot of heat and dust—but there's no sand in my eyes!'

Coda

Durga Shakti's suspension, and the subsequent national movement which built up, had a spin-off effect. Under the public glare, the illegal sand mining came to a sudden halt. The National Green Tribunal stepped in and issued several strict advisories and directives against the practice across the country. There was a sea change, and the sand mafia found it impossible to work under the new policy. The banks of river Yamuna, and other rivers, were saved from further degradation due to the illegal process.

Civil society and the media were sensitized to the pressure under which civil servants worked. Due to Noida's closeness to the national capital, they had seen Durga Shakti's fight against the unlawful mafia, and the stress and strain owing to the system, from close quarters. They recognized that perhaps other officers had been serving in remoter parts of the country, and doing incredible work, under similar pressure for years—without any recognition.

Durga Shakti grew stronger with the experience. Even when she was overtaken by intense anguish, there was no confusion or conflict in her mind. There were no regrets. Now, she looks back with satisfaction, and is happy that she was neither disconcerted nor deterred by her experience. Seven years later, although she has not returned to Uttar Pradesh since, she continues to work with the same zeal to preserve the rule of law in the Government of India.

VII

Computers and Viruses

If you have patience and belief in yourself,
the goal is not too far . . .

'Strike! Strike! Strike!'

Anita looked out of the glass panel in her office. She was surprised to see a group of angry-looking men outside the cabin of the Managing Director of the Central Cottage Industries Corporation of India Limited (CCIC). The inauguration of the computerization project was over. Anita had walked into her workplace after seeing the Chief Guest off. As she lowered herself into the office chair, she breathed a sigh of relief.

'A job well done,' the Cabinet Secretary, the Chief Guest, had said.

'Indeed—great work,' the Chairman of the Board had concurred.

Anita had beamed and sighed with a deep sense of satisfaction. The task had been tough; the effort enormous.

Her pet project had been approved by the board in the face of strong opposition six months ago. 'What an uphill task that was,' Anita thought. 'It's now time to celebrate.'

She picked up the intercom and called her private secretary, Madan. 'Please arrange for a cake and some coffee, Madan. Call the core team of the project for a celebration.'

Anita heard a click at the other end. Instead of responding, Madan walked into her office, looking flustered. He sported a frown and said something that startled her. 'They came in when you went to see the Chief Guest off, and wrote their demands on this paper. They are planning a strike, ma'am.'

'What! Who is?' Anita asked angrily, pacing up and down the office.

'The Employees Union, ma'am. All the employees have joined in. As we speak, they have planted a red flag announcing the strike, and are having a "gate meeting" at the main entrance.'

Anita flopped down in her chair. The state of elation she was in a few minutes ago disappeared. 'Good Lord! A strike? But why?'

'Who knows, ma'am? They say it's the computerization programme, but they have complicated matters by adding all sorts of other grievances to their list of demands.'

Anita frowned. She felt rather let down. This, after two years of herculean efforts to put the CCIC back on track! Despite all the problems besetting it, they were no longer in the red. Things were looking up now. As the Managing Director (MD) of the CCIC, Anita had worked long hours to make that happen.

Two years ago, on a pleasant day in August 1996, she had walked into the beautiful office of the Managing Director of the CCIC, with mixed feelings. She was delighted that she had got the job. It would enable her to stay with her husband and children in Delhi for two more years. Her husband's work required him to be in the city. The children were too young to be without their mother, and too old to keep changing schools.

There was a sense of achievement, for she had been appointed as the MD after a rather tough selection process. At the same time, she was apprehensive. She was aware that she was up against a difficult situation. She was the first IAS officer to be the MD of an organization that was wary and unaccepting of an outsider.

The affairs of the CCIC were not in order. In 1996, it was no longer the organization it had been decades ago. The leading role of the Cottage Emporium was challenged by the state emporia. They were keen competitors for the same clientele. The carefully selected employees of Cottage Emporium had become highly unionized. The trade unions were strong. The connect with artisans had grown weak. Sales were declining. Expenses needed to be controlled. And, over the years, apathy had set in. There was a great deal to be done.

For the last two years, Anita had worked hard to motivate her team and strengthened the contact with the artisans. She had helped new procedures evolve, made processes more transparent, and upgraded existing systems using technology. Finally, the Cottage Emporium was back on a growth trajectory. Anita brought a personal touch to the workplace.

She knew the members of the staff by name, and had built a rapport with the employees. Or so she had thought.

And here she was, alone in her room while her entire staff was on a strike against the computerization project that had just been inaugurated. They were protesting against her. The reason behind the call for a strike by the Employees Union was the recent introduction of computers to smoothen the functioning of the CCIC.

Anita felt rather disillusioned. She had struggled against the inherent propensity of an organization to avoid change— any change—by going slow and taking everyone along. Computerization of the organization had posed an additional challenge of changing the management within the CCIC.

In the 1990s, computers were a new animal in the government. A lot of unfounded fears needed to be allayed— of the computers replacing humans and, consequently, large-scale-retrenchment. There was even an irrational rumour amongst the junior employees that needed to be busted: 'Computers get infected with a virus that can also infect the person using the machines.'

The decision to computerize all the departments of the CCIC rose from a problem posed to Anita one morning almost eight months ago. Madan brought a pleasant, young sales girl into the MD's office. The poor girl looked tense. She stood half hidden behind him.

'Madam, this is Seema. She works in the emporium and wants to talk to you,' he said, introducing the nervous girl.

'Please help me, madam. I did not do anything wrong. It's not my fault,' Seema begged her, with tears in her eyes.

Anita offered the flustered girl a chair. 'Sit down. Have a glass of water. And now tell me what happened. Nothing can be so bad.'

'Madam, I can't pay the entire amount at one go. It is too much. Who can afford to pay Rs 5800 at once? It's too much for me, madam,' Seema said between sobs.

Anita was perplexed. She looked up at her Secretary, who was still standing at the back of the room staring at the distraught girl.

He came forward and explained the situation. 'Madam, she undercharged a customer for an item. The accounts department discovered an error of Rs 5,800, and have decided to deduct it from her salary. The HR department has been informed. They are planning an enquiry into the matter.'

'It was a mistake, ma'am. I didn't do it on purpose,' Seema interjected.

'She has requested that the recovery of the amount from her salary should be done in instalments.' Madan pressed the girl's case.

'Please help me, madam!' Seema urged her.

Anita looked at Seema's pale face.

'Ma'am, please believe me, it was a genuine mistake—a human error.'

The words 'human error' stayed with Anita. Making recoveries for shortfall from a salesperson's salary was a rule in the organization Anita had recently introduced. After meeting Seema, she was convinced that the girl had not taken the money for herself. The root cause of the problem possibly lay elsewhere. She consulted her colleagues and realized that a systemic change to reduce human error was needed immediately. Merely making recoveries was not a lasting solution.

Of late, the problem of incorrect billing had been on the rise. The footfall in the Cottage Emporium showrooms had increased due to the effective changes Anita's team had brought about in various sectors such as designing, procurement, marketing, pricing, and display. With the improved footfall, the problem of incorrect billing had increased. It was an inefficient system. There were long queues of customers waiting for their bills. Discrepancies in the preparation of the bills had grown. Undercharging and incorrect billing for goods had become rampant—sometimes through carelessness and sometimes by design. The amounts involved were not small and could not be ignored. In one instance, a Maharashtrian paithani sari costing Rs 1,00,000 was billed for Rs. 10,000 by a salesperson, who claimed that the omission of a zero, while preparing the bill, was a genuine 'human error', thereby causing a loss of Rs 90,000 to the company.

Anita's new rule of deducting the difference in the amount from the salesperson's salary had made a difference. It was better than suspending the employee. But it had not quite sorted the matter out. As she sat pondering over a permanent solution to the problem of incorrect billing, Seema's worried face came to her mind. Something had to be done to reduce human errors.

And then she had looked up with a broad smile on her face. 'The time is ripe to computerize the working of the CCIC, and to put my knowledge to use.'

A few years earlier, in 1990, she had attended a government-sponsored master's programme in Information Technology at the University of Birmingham. The course was hectic and required twelve hours of work a day, for over five months. Armed with information about the latest technology, Anita had returned to India all set to bring about changes in the government. She had had to wait a few years before she could apply the knowledge she had gained. Now, as the Managing Director of the CCIC, it was time to put her knowledge to good use.

Computerization of the existing systems at the CCIC would benefit the staff, bring in greater efficiency, cut down errors, and give a professional image to the company. The customer interface would improve, as it would benefit the clients and curtail delays.

Anita had discussed the proposal, individually and collectively, with the senior officers of the company. All the divisions were enthusiastic and had lent wholehearted support. The finance unit was headed by Pramod Nagpal, a competent and unassuming Chartered Accountant, who saw merit in the idea. He became Anita's greatest ally in the computerization plan over the next six months.

A stakeholder consultation at all levels of the organization was essential. Every day, Anita and a core team conducted meetings with all the units of the CCIC administration, sales, stores, procurement and finance. They were taken through the need for computerization in their respective division, the system, the process and the positive impact it would have on their functioning. Several meetings were held with the staff unions and other stakeholders.

Everyone was on board. There was an air of excitement. After the stakeholder consultations, it was decided to barcode all artefacts and goods in the emporia for efficient and correct billing. An extensive programme for training the staff, without hampering the sales, was conducted. The officers were also trained along with the staff. Everyone was enthused by the idea. During the training, there was a sense of camaraderie. It appeared that everyone felt that the computerization project was theirs.

After the buy-in by the staff and officers, the next hurdle to be crossed was the project approval by the board of directors. A representative of the Textile Ministry was the government's nominee. He pulled out a long list of queries from his briefcase with a grim face:

'Will computerization be useful? If so, how?'

'How will you ensure that it is not merely wasteful expenditure?'

'Will the expenditure be worth the effort?'

So on and so forth.

Anita had taken a deep breath and started responding. This was going to be a long day—almost as long as the stakeholder consultation with the Union Leaders. Her mind went back to an afternoon when a Union Member had also pulled out a similar list of questions from his pocket:

'So, why should we agree to computers?'

'How will you ensure that the computers won't take our jobs away?

'How will you ensure that a computer virus won't infect an employee?'

'What compensation will be paid if the virus infects a user?'

Anita had managed to convince both—the Union and the board—about the efficacy of the use of computers to improve the work environment at the CCIC. After the board's approval, work on the computerization project had started in earnest. The journey was long and arduous. Several milestones were reached along the way: the purchase of hardware, the writing of software, the meticulous training of the staff, the successful testing of each segment of the software and the renovation of the interiors. Everything went as planned. The hard work put in by the officers and the staff paid off. Six months later, the project was ready for inauguration.

The Cabinet Secretary had been invited as the chief guest. There was much fanfare and jubilation. A press note was prepared and released. Everybody congratulated each other. Anita was on top of the world. She had no idea about what lay in store for her once the inaugural ceremony was over.

'The staff refuses to work, madam. They have all gone on strike,' said Madan.

Just then Pramod Nagpal, Finance Manager, walked in and said, 'I just met Beer Singh, the Union Leader. He is not willing to budge. Not an inch.'

'But they were all there at the inauguration. How could they suddenly change stance within a couple of hours?' Anita asked.

'It doesn't seem to be a sudden decision. I think it was planned well in advance. They were merely playing along this morning, waiting for the inaugural function to be over,' Pramod Nagpal opined.

'That seems right, madam. When Beer Singh came to drop the list of demands in my room, he said—and I quote: "The MD earned her points, so we attended the inauguration to let her go on. But there is nothing in it for us . . ." The others cheered him on.' Madan looked embarrassed.

'What a dreadful finale to a successful project,' Anita sighed.

'All aspects of the project were taken into account. The entire staff was kept on board at every stage. If they refuse to work now, the entire project will be reduced to naught,' she said sadly.

Bad news poured in all day. Anita paced the floor, thinking about what had gone wrong.

'We have had to shut the showroom down, madam. There is no one to man the counters,' the showroom manager came in to say. 'The salespersons have left. Customers are standing around with no one to attend to them.'

Anita called some of her close confidantes from amongst the staff to understand the issue. Individually, they claimed that they were with the MD but showed reluctance to go against the Union. It was time to invite the Union Leaders for a discussion. The leaders entered the MD's office, full of self-importance, led by the burly and aggressive Beer Singh.

'Madam, we supported you over this project through these last few months because we thought you would provide something for us too. As far as you are concerned, you have completed your "pet project" and will go away on a new posting. But the staff will have to work extra hard on these

computers for years to come. What benefit is there for them?'
he said.

'You know, we have learnt that computers have some
virus. What if we also get the virus? What will happen to our
children?' said the frail-looking Masterji—the man who had
asked her the same question six months ago.

'But I explained to you it's not possible . . .' Anita started
to explain.

'That may be so, madam, but we still need compensation.
Even the government gives a computer allowance for
operating computers,' another person interrupted her.

'Yes,' said Beer Singh. 'We thought you would announce
a hefty allowance for us today at the inaugural function.
Madam, we are very disappointed. You have given us nothing.
And a strike is our answer!'

'Strike! Strike! Strike!' The others cheered.

Anita was in no mood to plead with them. She was not
willing to be blackmailed into allowing any 'computer-' or
'virus allowance'. The meeting ended in a deadlock. The
union leaders left in a huff.

'This is going to be a long haul,' she said, as they left.

The prospect of keeping the showroom closed loomed
large. Pramod looked concerned, for the Cottage Emporium
on Janpath was the face of the CCIC.

The showroom manager suggested a possible solution:

'Let us ask the officers to run the showroom for a while.
I am certain we'll find some who will volunteer to do it.'

The ratio of staff to officers at the CCIC was 70:30. This
sounded like a good idea.

'Suppose they, too, join the strike?' Anita wondered aloud.

'No, madam, they cannot. The officers of a company can only form an association. However, they cannot go on strike.'

'Good! So let us call an emergency meeting. I will talk to them and seek their assistance.'

She looked around the room. She could see that some of the officers were sympathetic and showed their willingness to help out. Some looked amused. Still others had a look on their faces that seemed to say, 'So, what will you do next? Let us see you get out of this predicament.'

Anita ignored the defiant look on those few faces. 'It takes all kinds to make the world after all,' she thought, as she addressed the group of officers at the CCIC. She said, 'Fate has given us this opportunity to prove ourselves. CCIC has given all of us gathered here today respect, gratification, and our livelihoods. It needs us. It is now our time—yours and mine—to give back to an organization that has given us so much. All those who would like to give back to the Cottage Emporium family in its time of need—please stay. The others may leave.'

Not a single person walked out of the meeting. The showroom opened the next day as usual. But the sales counters were manned by officers of the CCIC—accountants, designers, computer programmers, administrators and others.

The staff union was perturbed. Their plan to blackmail the MD and bring the management to its knees was in danger. The Union leaders gathered at the gate of the emporium and started raising slogans. They stopped the customers from entering the showroom.

Anita called the Police Commissioner, a batchmate who had trained with her at Mussoorie. The police was very helpful. They moved the strikers across the road and drove them into a corner. They categorically informed the striking employees that they could not prevent the buyers from entering the showroom, and could only sit on the other side of the road.

The showroom started to work normally. In fact, it worked even better since the new system of computerized billing and other systems and processes also commenced simultaneously and provided greater customer satisfaction.

The finance and sales managers put together a roster so that work in the office did not suffer. Every two hours, the MD took a round of all the three floors of the showroom. She stopped by in the various sections to encourage the officers manning the counters. For five days, the emporium opened on time and the sales continued as usual. The customers were delighted by the enhanced efficiency and the reduced waiting time to pay their bills. No one could have guessed that there was any problem, but for the red flag and the group of Union leaders and picket sitting across the road behind a police barrier.

However, this arrangement could not go on forever. 'Sales' is a very specialized skill, and the managerial and administrative staff could not attain the heights of success that the Cottage Emporium salespersons usually did. The striking employees were also getting restive, since the work at the Cottage Emporium continued normally. Their strike was a failure—and they had little bargaining power to demand a computer allowance. Anita was certain that they would approach the management for negotiations soon. However, the leaders were stubborn and did not send out any feelers even on the fifth day of the strike.

Anita decided to make the first move. She called in Anand Lakhotia, her seasoned Manager, Administration. 'Computerization seems to have shown us that we are overstaffed. The showroom is doing quite well. Sales, too, are not hampered. Let us start retrenching some of the staff.'

He looked at her incredulously. He had never thought that the mild-tempered MD could be so ruthless. Before he could react, Anita reminded him of the legal position. 'The staff has gone on strike without any formal notice. What they gave us is only a list of demands. This strike is illegal.'

'That's true, ma'am.' Anand Lakhotia found his tongue.

He was a cautious man. He never took hasty steps, and believed in maintaining the status quo. 'We will need to do a detailed work study analysis and—'

'Okay. Do an analysis—but a quick one. Draw up a list of the staff we do not really need,' Anita interrupted him before he could finish. And then she added after a pause, 'This strike has provided us the perfect opportunity to do away with dead wood.'

'That's true.'

Anita looked up at the door she had purposely left ajar. She sensed rather than saw animated faces taking in every word of her conversation with the manager. As expected, the 'secret discussions' between the manager, the administration, and the MD of the CCIC spread like wildfire. The epic 'secret discussion' had the desired effect. The next morning, on the sixth day of the strike, the Union leaders sent an emissary at 9.30 a.m. They requested a meeting.

The group, when they entered, were less arrogant and less sure of themselves than on the previous occasion when they had met the MD. Their list of demands had shortened to just one major appeal. 'All we want is a computer allowance. For the time being, just announce it—do not pay it—and we will resume work,' said the surly Beer Singh.

The rest of the management felt that was reasonable. But Anita was adamant. 'No. And no means no. There will be no computer allowance at the CCIC. I suggest you get that out of your head,' she said firmly. 'You may leave now.'

All the managers at the CCIC thought it was a wrong move. 'Ma'am, maybe we should reconsider it. All they want is a token amount and an announcement. Let them rejoin work first. We can always withdraw it later,' said the ever-cautious Anand, after the Union leaders had left.

Anita looked at the Finance Manager, who shook his head in agreement with her decision. They both knew that once a new head of account for an allowance was created in the public sector enterprise, it would be impossible to close it. If Anita had agreed, the CCIC would have had to face the prospect of increasing the amount of computer allowance paid to all the employees year after year.

'Anand, I know what I am doing. Please go ahead with the preparation of the list of staff to be retrenched,' Anita said firmly, knowing full well that there were eavesdroppers lurking in the corridor. 'I want to see that list on my desk latest by 8 p.m. tonight,' she emphasized, as he stood with the door ajar on his way out.

All that had transpired in the MD's office was shared across the corporation. There were all sorts of rumours afloat at the CCIC. Discussions were held in the corridors, the canteen, and near the water cooler. Most people were of the opinion that the MD was being too harsh. The CCIC was in for troubled times ahead.

But Anita did not relent. She went through the 'retrenchment list' sent to her that evening. Although she seemed to be in control, she had a rather troubled night with several anxious moments.

The next morning, the seventh day, dawned with a new sun. Beer Singh, the Union leader, asked for a personal meeting with her at 8.30 a.m., before the office opened officially.

Anita could sense the desperation in his voice. 'Madam, please understand. The entire staff looks up to me. What face will I show to them?'

He was no longer the burly, surly leader.

'That's your problem, not mine,' said Anita. She postured an inflexible stance, trying to gauge how far she could push him. She was buying time to see what the Union leader had up his sleeve.

'You are the mai-baap, MD Sahib. You cannot be so harsh. Are you serious about the retrenchment?'

'Yes, we are. I have the list right here. You know the strike is illegal. You gave us no notice. We shall now see you in court.'

Beer Singh looked up and, even before he spoke, Anita understood that the impasse was broken.

'Give me some face-saving, madam!'

Anita sat listening to him with a deadpan expression.

'I will call off the strike today only. Just help me. Give me a way out, please!' he pleaded.

He was obviously not aware that Anita was using the threat of retrenchment more as a bargaining tool than anything else.

'I am not willing to grant any computer allowance. Not a rupee,' she said.

Beer Singh looked at the MDs stern, blank face, as if looking for a chink in the armour. There seemed to be none.

'You know that the festival season has started. Diwali is just round the corner. It will be good if you all resume work, but that has to be unconditional.' As she said these words, she felt a flutter of anxiety.

The footfall in the showroom was increasing with the Festival of Lights drawing near. Maximum sales usually happened during this time of the year. The officers manning the sales counters were not skilled, and were getting weary. She knew that time was running out. The deadlock with the union had to be sorted out—and soon.

While these thoughts ran through her mind, her face remained impassive. 'Beer Singh must never know just how worried I am,' she thought, as she offered her adversary a cup of tea.

'Madam, I have come to you with folded hands. The employees are worried about the retrenchment. They are upset with me because the Union called for a strike without giving notice—and are threatening to leave it and go back to work.' Beer Singh looked rather desolate.

Anita was surprised and relieved at the cards Beer Singh had placed on the table. 'You must help me with some form of face-saving. Else the Union and I will become redundant.'

'Okay. Let me think. There is bound to be a solution, but no computer allowance.'

Anita smiled at Beer Singh for the first time since he had entered her office that morning.

The Trade Union at the CCIC had become strong over the years. Policies were often made keeping the Union in mind, including the granting of the festival bonus to the staff on Diwali each year. A month before the strike, Mukesh Mathur, the Finance Manager, had shown Anita the profits the Cottage Emporium had made so far, and had taken her verbal consent for a 10 per cent hike in the Diwali bonus that year. This was to be formalized and announced later. It was a major departure from the normal 5 to 6 per cent raise each year.

'There lies the solution to the deadlock,' Anita mused. As the Union leader finished his cup of tea, she turned to him and offered him some sweets. 'Happy Diwali,' she said. Then she offered a possible meeting point to Beer Singh, crossing her fingers under the table. 'So let's make this Diwali a very happy one for all of us. You, sir, must call off the strike. The management will offer everyone a huge Diwali bonus—much larger than last year's 5 per cent.'

'How large?' Beer Singh asked.

Name an amount you have never received before at the Cottage Emporium.'

'Six per cent?'

'Go higher.' Anita smiled, and offered some more Diwali sweets to put him at ease.

'Eight per cent?' Beer Singh asked, his eyes becoming bigger as he worked out what it meant in terms of rupees. It was a tidy sum.

'Start working by noon today—and we'll make it 10 per cent,' Anita said with a broad smile. 'But no computer allowance.'

'*Ten* per cent?' Beer Singh asked in amazement.

'That's double of what you got last year.'

'Yes, yes. That is good. I'll go out and tell the others. We'll start work—today only!'

The Finance Manager walked in as he heard the union leader say this. 'Happy Diwali,' he said, and he picked up a sweet from the plate.

'Happy Diwali, sir! Ten per cent bonus, sir!'

By this time it was already 9.30 a.m. The office was abuzz with the news of the meeting between the union leader and the MD. Everybody had been waiting with bated breath to know about the outcome of the negotiations.

'10 per cent Diwali bonus!' —a shout went up in the corridor.

The strike was called off. And Anita heaved a sigh of relief. The employees returned to work well before noon the same day. There was no more talk of a computer allowance at the Cottage Emporium ever again. No one ever talked about the virus that jumped from the computer to the user.

Coda

The Cottage Emporium, Delhi, a beautifully curated one-stop shopping centre for genuine handlooms and handicrafts of India, has been an icon at Janpath since 1952. The goods are sourced directly from artists and weavers. The quality of the goods, the exclusivity of the designs, the presentation of the products, and a unique marketing strategy, has helped the organization maintain a leading role in the market. Artisans and weavers are an integral part of the Cottage Emporium family.

Cottage Emporium grew and later developed into the CCIC, a Public Sector Undertaking, in 1976. The business expanded. New showrooms were set up in all the metros: Mumbai, Chennai, Hyderabad, Bangalore and Kolkata. It became more professional. Separate units were set up for the procurement of goods, stores, sales, marketing, finance, accounts, quality control, design, exports and even display. The staff strength multiplied. However, over time the revenues reduced, the expenditures kept increasing and the profitability declined. In 1996, when Anita took over as the Managing Director, the CCIC was in the red.

The evening the strike was called off, the showroom manager reported that a *pichwai* (cloth painting) priced at Rs 1,70,000 had been sold by a salesman who had been on the MD's 'fake retrenchment list', within a few hours of rejoining work. Each time Anita had passed the painting during the strike, she had wondered why it had not been sold. She had thought it was possibly overpriced, but the showroom manager was convinced that any person on his sales team would be able to sell it in no time. Her respect for the salespersons went up several notches.

The office staff went back to their respective divisions. Everyone was a winner.

Computerized billing, procurement, inventory and stocktaking became an intrinsic part of the functioning of the Cottage Emporia around the country. The CCIC became one of the few paperless offices in the government in the 1990s. Every member of the Cottage Emporium family became computer literate to some extent.

VIII

Flowering Success in the Land of the Rising Sun

For you are never given a dream . . .
without being given the ability to make it come true

'Get off that stool! Oiyao! Come down right now! Do you want to hurt yourself?' Emily Doley had a shock as she looked up from the shawl she was weaving. Through the window, she saw her daughter standing on a rickety old stool in the middle of the courtyard of their home in Sissibargaon in Dhemaji—on the northern bank of the river, Brahmaputra, in Assam, near the foothills of Arunachal Pradesh.

'Let the poor girl be, Herah! And what is "Oiyao"? Our daughter is all grown up now. Call her by her real name. What a beautiful name she has—Shakuntala,' L.K. Doley said with a laugh.

'Oiyao's Abo, my daughter will always be my little one—my Oiyao.'

'Yes, but she is practising hard for her interview for the civil services. You'll see. Soon our Oiyao will be an IAS officer—the very first girl from the Mishing Tribe!'

'I know she has these lofty dreams . . . and you—Oiyao's Abo—have been encouraging her. But I don't understand how her oratory skills will improve by making her stand on a stool to give speeches in English, and Hindi, and Assamese and . . . She will fall off that stool one day! And why so many languages?'

'O Herah! That is very important. Multilingualism can be a great binding force in a country as diverse and varied as ours. Also, God knows which part of the nation our Shakuntala will be serving. Soon she will be a Collector. Imagine that, Herah. Our dear Shakuntala will be the youngest girl to be a civil servant from the North-east . . .'

'Don't put all these fancy ideas into her head. Mishing girls don't become Collectors. They marry and look after their new homes. She is already twenty-two and should be learning how to cook and weave. And you, Oiyao's Abo, should be looking for a good boy to marry her off to before the monsoons arrive and the Brahmaputra is in spate,' Shakuntala's mother reminded her husband.

Shakuntala's face fell as Emily returned to her weaving. 'But, Baba, I have worked so hard. I have cleared the preliminary examination and the main exam too. Now only the interview is left. Being a civil servant is my dream.'

'A dream, my dear girl, is a great place to begin. Remember what Bach said?'

Both father and daughter laughed as they quoted in unison: 'You are never given a dream without being given the ability to make it come true!'

As she sat down on the chair of the Chief Secretary, Arunachal Pradesh, Shakuntala Doley Gamlin of the 1984 batch of the IAS, recalled that day distinctly. From where she sat in her office in Itanagar, her parents' home in the wetlands of the northern Brahmaputra Valley seemed far away.

'Look, Baba, I have gone way beyond becoming a Collector. Ma, your favourite Oiyao is now a Chief Secretary—the first girl from the Mishing tribe to be one,' Shakuntala whispered to the departed souls of her parents.

The role of the Chief Secretary, Arunachal Pradesh—the eastern-most part of India with an extensive international border—was rather challenging. The state covers a largely forested area of 84,000 square kilometres. The mountainous land shares international borders with Bhutan in the west, Myanmar in the east, and a disputed border with Tibet-China in the north, along the McMahon Line. In the south, it shares its borders with the states of Assam and Nagaland. Insurgency issues take a toll every now and then.

The terrain is by and large hilly in the south, but rapidly changed to a mountainous landscape, culminating at the crest of the eastern Himalayas in the north. In the southern region, the outskirts of the hills merge with the great alluvial northern plains of the Brahmaputra. Arunachal Pradesh is sparsely populated, and has a population density of about seventeen people per square kilometre, which is far below the Indian average of 370 per square kilometre elsewhere. The population comprises twenty-six major tribes and more than a 100 subtribes. The major tribes included the Adi (Abor), Aka, Apatani, Nyishi (Daffla), Tagin, Galo, Khampti, Bugun (Khowa), Mishmi, Momba (Monpa), Sherdukpen,

Singpho, Nocte, and Tangsa. Hindi is the lingua franca, and consequently the link language within the state.

Shakuntala Doley had married Jarbom Gamlin, a young student leader from the Galo Tribe of Arunachal Pradesh. She had met and married him when they were in college in Delhi. As a young bride, she had visited his home in Village Aalo near Pasighat and Lekabali for the first time. She had fallen in love with the beautiful land her husband hailed from. She did not know that one day she would wind up as the first woman Chief Secretary of the state, a Chief Secretary who left behind footprints—some that were tangible and others that were more amorphous and enduring.

Of the tangible achievements, Shakuntala's top priority was infrastructure and connectivity by way of roads, bridges and airports. Infrastructure was inadequate and, at times, completely lacking. Rail and air connectivity were limited. Road connectivity was suboptimal. Bridges and roads took much longer than scheduled, due to inordinate delays. The quality of construction was poor. As the head of the administration, she ensured that a road map was prepared to build strategic infrastructure as well as to enhance connectivity within the state.

Although infrastructure was not the direct responsibility of a Chief Secretary, Shakuntala monitored the department's progress on a regular basis, and toured the region regularly for inspections. Stumbling blocks were removed. She focused on sorting out problems that had occurred in the past and slowed down the progress of the work. Road development was given a push, especially the East-West Highway. The

Bogibeel Bridge across the Brahmaputra was completed expeditiously during her tenure. Shakuntala took up matters regarding the completion of the State Secretariat building in hand, and ensured that it was completed in less than a year.

Itanagar only had a helipad, but no airport for operating fixed-wing passenger and cargo aircrafts. Shakuntala identified a suitable site for an airport at Holonghi. Fortunately, the majority of the land required for the airport belonged to the state government and did not necessitate land acquisition. Necessary statutory clearances were obtained quickly for the civil work to start. Passenger flights were introduced to and from Pasighat, a town close to the Assam border. In addition, the Central government agreed to permit the use of the seven advance landing grounds meant for military aircraft, for the civil aircraft.

The need for Arunachal to have a medical college of its own continued to occupy Shakuntala's attention. Aware that it was not the easiest of tasks, she followed the proposal with far-off Delhi on a daily basis. With great effort, a medical college was sanctioned for Itanagar. Now it operates under the name of Tomo Riba Institute of Medical Sciences and Research (TRIMS). It is attached to the existing government hospital and is a boon for the state.

The modern Secretariat, the roads, the airport and TRIMS are the tangible symbols of Shakuntala's efforts to make a difference. She also undertook an important and life-altering journey that impacted the lives of those who were close to the ground—the Arunachali farmers.

Arunachal Pradesh had an abundance of unique and varied flora and fauna. Several large rivers flowed across from Tibet longitudinally to join the Brahmaputra. Besides gifting the state with an untapped hydropower potential of about 50,000 megawatts, almost one-third of India's potential, the rivers provided adequate irrigation. The soil and the climate were extremely suitable for ensuring a good harvest. Never had nature bestowed so much bounty upon one place.

What perplexed Shakuntala when she joined the state was why suitable agrarian and agri-marketing policies were not in place. Horticulture and marketing of organically farmed produce had not been attempted seriously. Nature's gifts in the form of good soil conditions, abundant water and a nurturing climate, could well provide socio-economic solutions to sustained development. The latter would provide succor to the tribal population.

Bio-diversity was maintained in the state since the climate changed after every 50 kilometres. At some places, even more dramatically. The climate in the extreme north-eastern state of the country varied between subtropical and tropical to temperate. With so much diversity, choices too abounded with what could, or ought to be, done to raise the standard of living of the people. The urgent need to protect the rich biodiversity beckoned Shakuntala.

The beautiful Rhododendron wardii, a yellow-flower tree, was unique to Arunachal. Plant hunters like Francis Kingdon Ward had discovered extremely rare plant species like the Himalayan blue poppy or meconopsis betonicifolia, and primula florinade, named after his first wife, or the giant cowslip, during the first quarter of the twentieth century. Furthermore, Arunachal was home to over 600 of the 1,200-odd orchid species found in the country. The eagle-eyed gaze of Kingdon Ward had not fallen on the rich treasure of exotic orchids growing in the wild.

The orchid census conducted by the Botanical Survey of India revealed the rare and rich heritage of the state.

'Our orchids have to be given the importance they deserve,' Shakuntala thought. She toured the territory widely, and visited the richest concentration of orchids at Tipi in Bhalukpong, the Ziro Valley, and also along the foothills bordering Assam.

'Unfortunately, time appears to be running out. Many varieties of orchid have already become endangered on account of encroachment of their habitat.' Shakuntala was informed about the situation by Tomo Jarken, the Director of Agriculture, accompanying her on the tour.

The state had an Orchid Research Centre with orchid-specialists in Tippi in West Kameng district. The first thing Shakuntala did was to nurture the institute and involve the specialists in developing a State Orchid Development Plan. To begin with, a sensitization campaign was started. Local people were sensitized towards the need to observe caution in dealing with orchids.

'Our people may not even need the sensitization training, madam,' said Sonam Wangdi, the orchid expert.

'Why is that?' Shakuntala asked him.

'The fact is that the Arunachalis, especially the tribals, have learnt to coexist with nature. Their knowledge regarding useful plants—whether for food or medicinal use—is truly stupendous! They respect the flora and their environment.'

'You are right. The people possess an earthy wisdom. My father-in-law, a political interpreter during British India, once told me an interesting story. A Bada Sahib happened to ask someone from a village he visited about the dust on his clothes. The reply he received could set anyone thinking for a very long time.'

'What was the reply, Ma'am?'

'Well, he heard: "Sir, dirt is a poor man's clothing. It protects him from the elements and the poisonous creatures in the jungles." And that left the Bada Shib open-mouthed.'

'I can imagine that, madam!' He laughed at the image in his mind.

'Our people have got used to a certain way of living with minimal needs—a form of joyous subsistence . . .' Shakuntala responded with a smile.

'Sadly, in terms of family income, the position appears to have remained the same as what existed so many years ago. Especially, in some of the remote unconnected villages, things are really bad. Something has to be done— and done right now—to raise the living standards of the Arunachalis.'

Several brainstorming sessions were conducted with the stakeholders to reap the potential benefits of orchid cultivation effectively, as a means to improve livelihoods. At the beginning, Shakuntala laid down the conditions. 'Let us all think of ways to save the endangered orchids, as we think of means to improve the lot of the Arunachalis. Please make your suggestions freely. However, I would like to stipulate something. Whatever effort is proposed to protect the endangered orchid varieties must not come at the cost of livelihoods of an already impoverished people.'

'Yes, madam. Taking up from what Madam Chief Secretary has said, I think we need to look at out-of-the-box solutions. Let us induct people as partners in the venture. Their role should not be limited to protection alone, but should also extend to improving livelihoods,' said Tomo Jarken, Director, Agriculture.

'Why not ask people to grow orchids in baskets in their homes, with family support?' suggested Sonam Wangdi of the Orchid Research Centre at Tippi.

'That's a great idea.' Shakuntala smiled. 'I recall you once told me how all Arunachalis are environment friendly and how they inherently respect the flora around them.'

'Indeed, they respect the flora, but they cannot be expected to become either connoisseurs or saviours of flowers essentially sought by the affluent. They would need intensive training,' said Jarter Riba, a horticulture specialist in the Arunachal government.

'What do you suggest, Sonam?' Shakuntala asked, turning to the orchid expert.

The young botanist beamed, and was encouraged to share another idea. 'We could have a group of aggregators who will purchase the orchids and deliver them to the nearest airport,' he said.

'But they are so delicate and fragile! Won't we lose out if they don't sell?' asked a concerned farmer.

'Well, you needn't worry about the marketing. A seasonal rate will be fixed for different varieties. The aggregators will collect them from the growers once they've grown,' Sonam replied.

'Yes, but they *are* delicate! Certainly, they must have a short shelf life. Suppose they wilt before they can be picked up from the farmer and transported?' asked a prospective aggregator.

'Orchids appear delicate, but are relatively hardy when compared with other flowers. They have a shelf life extending up to ten days,' said the Director of the Tippi Institute.

After that, there seemed to be a great deal of excitement when the numbers and financials were discussed. Following some friendly wrangling, a few varieties were identified for growing in baskets at home including the cymbidium, phalaenopsis, dendrobium, and , and paphiopedilum.

'Great. So here is our opportunity to help farmers, and even housewives, improve their living standards,' Shakuntala said to the stakeholders around the table.

'Madam, I volunteer to help spread the message across to various stakeholders in the community and popularize the idea,' Mr Ralom from Pasighat offered. He was a rather dedicated member of civil society. He played a key role in the spreading of the orchid project, which provided additional income to the stakeholders and improved their financial condition.

Matters did not end with orchids. An exotic fruit—the blueberry—was found, quite by chance, to be growing in the wild in West Kameng district. On a visit to an Indo Tibetan Border Police (ITBP) camp, Shakuntala Gamlin was shown some photographs. One of the photographs depicted deep purplish-blue dots scattered on a bed of green foliage.

One question led to another till it was confirmed that the blue dots were indeed the edible blueberry, believed to be a native of the western hemisphere. Further search led to the discovery of blueberries growing in the wild. The matter was taken up with the Deputy Commissioner, West Kameng district, Sonal Swaroop, a young and enthusiastic officer, who became an immediate convert to the idea of propagating the growing of blueberries in the district. A nursery was soon established, and reports started to trickle in suggesting that the experiment appeared to have taken off.

Soon the returns from orchid cultivation and blueberry farming in West Kameng became a reason for other farmers to take up the activity. Local markets could, in no way, provide the correct value to the produce. Transporting the orchids and the berries to markets in metropolitan cities by air was an essential prerequisite to the success of the endeavour. With increased air traffic, Shakuntala widened the scope of the livelihood venture to include organic farming.

'What we need is an imaginative, courageous and purposeful approach, and the rest will fall into place,' Shakuntala reflected.

Identifying, formulating, and implementing the organic farming project was the next dream she worked on. In Arunachal, where man and nature have coexisted in a harmonious manner since the beginning, advocating the idea of producing food with natural fertilizers and pesticides, was not as difficult as one might have imagined.

'In Sikkim, a sister state, organic farming has become a fairly successful business. It provides decent dividends to the farmers. So why would it not take off here, in Arunachal

Pradesh, where conditions are, by and large, similar? In fact, even more favourable?' Shakuntala asked her team.

The team had done wonders with the Orchid Project. They were just as excited about the new challenge thrown at them by their Chief Secretary—the lady-on-the-go—as they had now started thinking of her. As always, there was a surfeit of ideas as to what ought to be grown, where and how. Every idea was examined, and sieved through, and a shortlist of potential and promising farmers and stakeholders was prepared, with the involvement of the concerned departments and district officials.

Shakuntala did not want to spread the team members too thin. Any initial failure in a new venture was viewed harshly and, quite often, the baby was thrown out with the bath water. They finally decided to pick one produce and make it a success with end-to-end tie-ups. Once the product and the market had stabilized, then other vegetables and grains could be taken up.

The choice was narrowed down to three varieties of sticky rice native to Arunachal—white, brown, and black. The cultivation and marketing of all the three varieties expanded to several districts. This excellent organic rice compared with the best Jasmine rice from Thailand. The next step was to obtain its geographical indication. Before that could be done, Shakuntala was transferred to the Government of India. However, at present, the cultivation of organic white, brown, and black sticky rice continues. Efforts to obtain the geographical indication, and to have it labelled appropriately, are underway.

Shakuntala Doley Gamlin is no longer the Chief Secretary of Arunachal Pradesh, but she dreams that one day 'when the needs of Arunachal Pradesh are met, organic sticky rice will be available elsewhere in the country and abroad . . . that the orchids from Arunachal Pradesh will be the flowers of choice across the world . . . and that these and other dreams she has for Arunachal Pradesh will come true, 'for you are never given a dream without being given the ability to make it come true.'

Coda

Shakuntala Doley Gamlin has held a variety of posts in the Arunachal Pradesh-Goa-Mizoram and Union Territory (AGMUT) cadre from a district Assistant Commissioner to Chief Secretary.

She superannuated as Secretary, Department for Empowerment of Persons with Disabilities, with the Government of India. She took several initiatives towards inclusive education, early intervention, infrastructure accessibility, and Information Technology. She has contributed to setting up the Mental Health Rehabilitation Institute in Madhya Pradesh, focused upon developing a Mental Health Rehabilitation Programme, and has also introduced a Mental Health Help line throughout the country for identification, early intervention, and counselling.

Her time in the Industries and Finance Departments in Delhi was very rewarding. In the Industries Department she undertook various initiatives, transformed systems, procedures, and processes, through meticulous planning, teamwork, and precision in execution. As a result, the ranking of the Union Territory on the World Bank's Ease-of-Doing-Business scale, jumped seventy-two places.

Shakuntala is of the view that she was among the fortunate few to have been provided an opportunity to put in her best in the service of the nation. Upon retirement now, she plans to learn Sanskrit and improve her piano-playing skills. She would like to pick up threads where she left them, and go back to help expand orchid and organic farming in Arunachal Pradesh.

IX

Kanooni Bibi and the Panchayat Elections

*Rule of law and a yardstick
that's fair and universally applicable . . .*

'Panchayat elections are like a daughter's wedding . . . and
the Returning Officer (RO) is the parent of the bride.' Anjali
Chugh recalled, with acute clarity, the words of a seasoned
tehsildar who had helped conduct umpteen polls in Punjab.
It was 1983, and Punjab had announced panchayat elections
after many years. Anjali, the Sub-Divisional Magistrate (SDM)
had been declared the RO of a subdivision situated along the
Indo-Pak border, covering all the 600 plus panchayats in the
subdivision.

Free and fair elections are the very foundation of a
democracy. In India, panchayat elections are very keenly
contested and are critical to the democratic process. All the
candidates are well known to the electorate. The issues at
hand are close to every voter. Elections to the Parliament
and the assembly are extremely important, but the emotions

of a voter in the hinterland are not as intense as they are in the panchayat elections. These elections are linked to self-determination at the cutting edge level.

Elections are always a period of great activity and pressure. The buck stops at the RO, who has the ultimate responsibility. A Collector usually is declared as the RO for parliamentary and assembly elections. The SDM is normally the RO for the elections of local bodies like panchayats and municipalities.

Panchayat elections too need special attention with regard to law and order. Even a small incident can spark violence across the state, if not prudently nipped in the bud. The RO usually wears a dozen different hats Maintenance of law and order is an integral part of her responsibility as an SDM, making the RO nearly solely responsible for ensuring the conduct of a peaceful poll.

The year the panchayat elections were announced in Punjab, the state was battling against militancy. Indeed, the 1980s were a traumatic decade for the state. Anjali had recently joined her first posting as the SDM of Gurdaspur when the elections were announced.

Gurdaspur was a largely rural and agrarian district, sharing a border with the states of Jammu and Kashmir and Himachal Pradesh in the north and Pakistan in the west. Besides matters related to law and order, Anjali found that her job entailed a larger commitment to development works, requiring her to travel frequently.

The court work was heavy too—not only because Gurdaspur was a large subdivision, but also because it was a litigation-prone area. Land was the most important asset.

A large part of the populace was constantly at loggerheads with each other or with the state. Apart from an appreciable number of cases that went to the civil and criminal courts, many conflicting claims concerning land came to the SDM's revenue court.

A lawyer handling criminal cases gave Anjali an insight into the pugnacity prevalent in the area. He told her that the number of murder and assault cases could easily keep 'a sizable number of legal professionals busy through the year'. He confided that once when he had turned down a request to defend an accused in a murder case, the litigant had tried to persuade him to take it up, with an unusual argument.

'Vakeel Sahab, please take this case. You will not regret it. There is soon going to be another murder in the village. We'll bring that case to you too.' Clearly, on offer was a 'long-term arrangement on a permanent basis!'

Anjali foresaw a busy time ahead of her, and some valuable learning opportunities, despite the volatility of the situation. Law and order in Gurdaspur, the vulnerable border district, remained a matter of serious concern in 1983 with militancy at its peak. The added stress of the panchayat elections could only aggravate the situation.

The day the elections were announced, Anjali recalled the words of the tehsildar who had trained her during her attachment with the *tehsil* office during her district training. He had explained the election-related processes and procedures, and had also shared ground realities and warned her of several potential pitfalls. 'It is a herculean task. Your election manuals should be like a Bible. Every element is important and needs to be taken care of at the right time.

The procedure is sacrosanct. Even a seemingly unimportant task can prove to be critical and can vitiate the election.'

'There seems much to plan and prepare for,' Anjali had noted.

'Yes. Believe me, not only do you have to be meticulous, but also have to have your wits about you at all times. Else something or the other is bound to go wrong.'

Anjali had heard her trainer with concern, and mild disbelief, as he had listed out everything that could go wrong.

'Only after the election results are duly signed and declared can the "father of the bride", the harassed RO, breathe a sigh of relief—like after the *doli* (the palanquin) of the bride has departed.'

Anajali scrutinized the election manuals for the third time, and put a to-do list together for herself. The panchayat elections were less than a month away. There was a great deal to do besides discharging her regular duties— that kept an SDM on her toes. So here she was—preparing for a hotly contested election where anything could spark off a violent confrontation in her subdivision, where the public was highly litigious, at a time when the district was vulnerable to attacks by terrorists. There were intelligence reports that the militants were looking for opportunities to foment trouble.

Anjali drew a deep breath as she saw that her list of essential tasks for the elections ran into five pages and sixty-eight bullet points. The first thing on the list was the need to update the electoral rolls. The task was urgent and large. The next was taking stock of the law-and-order situation. She and the Deputy Superintendent of Police (DSP) conducted a detailed exercise to identify potential sources of aggravation.

The DSP, Gurpal Bal, who headed the police machinery of Gurdaspur sub-division, was a good twenty years older than her. He had worked in the state for many years, and had been in Gurdaspur for two years before she arrived. Gurpal Bal knew the area and the people of the subdivision well. He was an experienced officer—somewhat gruff, but not unkind. He managed to defer her judgement while skillfully guiding her.

The stocktaking was a sobering exercise. Both the SDM and the DSP realized the need for accurate and up-to-date intelligence at all times, so as to have the opportunity to craft an appropriate response. From his experience, Gurpal said that they needed advance information to enable them to put the kibosh on any incipient violence.

'Madam, I see you are a very calm and collected person normally . . . but panchayat elections are vexing. We should stop ourselves from overreacting to small issues. Often our overreaction itself might become a trigger for unrest.'

'I agree. The last thing we want is to appear out of control, DSP Sahab,' said Anjali.

'The trouble is that often there is insufficient information available to decide whether a situation requires a simple talking-through or a more robust response. At times like that, one has to feel one's way through gradually. The first important thing to do is to defuse the situation,' Gurpal reflected.

Anjali made a mental note of these words of experience.

The days were busy, interesting and challenging, but the evenings were lonesome. Anjali missed her conversations with her parents. Her father's advice had helped her through many a difficult problem in the past. She also missed her mother's manner of putting things in perspective—often with a down-to-earth and unexpected twist.

Anjali smiled as she remembered a conversation. She had been venting her resentment against a senior colleague while chatting with her father. Her mother, shelling peas nearby and listening to them, had intervened and provided a charming insight.

'What did you say his name was? Which part of the country is he from?' she had asked.

'I'm not sure, Mama. Probably Odisha. Why do you ask?'

'Poor boy. So far from home . . . maybe that's why he is not so nice to people.'

'Should that matter? He's forty years old!'

'Yes, but the poor thing is so far away from his mother!'

After that, it became impossible to feel upset or threatened by a person who was rudderless because he lacked his 'mother's guiding hand'. Each time the senior officer was rude, Anjali was unruffled, remembering her mother's words: 'He's possibly missing his mother . . .'

Before she slept, Anjali often wished her parents were with her with their warm affection and advice that helped reset perspectives. In addition to the many challenges expected in a new job, the panchayat elections and the associated law-and-order problems weighed heavily on her mind. She was aware that no one would pat her for a job done well but, if anything went wrong, her reputation would suffer and she herself would feel a failure.

As the polls approached, Anjali and the DSP met more often to chalk out their plans for a smooth event. They identified villages in the subdivision that needed closer monitoring: large villages, those with a history of simmering acrimony, villages with recent crimes, and those with bellicose candidates or candidates with criminal records. They established appropriate standard operating procedures (SOPs), and drilled them down to field officers from the police and revenue departments.

Together they visited the sensitive villages and held meetings. They were treated with courtesy. Anjali learnt to explain the legal rights and responsibilities of the electorate to the subdivisional officers and the public. She also did her best to convey a firm message that indiscipline and unlawful behaviour would not be tolerated.

She spoke to large gatherings in chaste Punjabi with an urban accent, she wondered whether her audience had faith in one so young and inexperienced. Moreover, one who was an outsider to the subdivision. 'They are all much older than I am and have known many previous SDMs. I wonder what they make of my accent and my lack of years. I hope I can build faith in my ability to manage things.'

While she worked hard to develop confidence in her magisterial capabilities, she began to settle down in her allotted house with her household possessions comprising four folding chairs, a tiny refrigerator and a folding bed. There was no time or money to add to the basics. Touring and understanding the subdivision, and pronouncing and writing court judgements, took up a great deal of her time each day. Sundays were reserved for reading up for the cases in court. The days hurtled by—each one busy, with a great deal to be done, and laws and developmental schemes to be absorbed and implemented. All through this, and not always in the background, there was the white noise of the panchayat polls which soon came upon her.

Everything else took a back seat as the bandobast (the arrangements for the elections) was put in place. A great deal of Anjali's time was taken up in settling complaints, and in the tedious process of finalizing the voluminous electoral rolls. She hoped she had given attention to every critical detail.

The complaints were predictable.

'Madam, he is trying to influence my polling agent!'

'No, madam, he has bought mine over!'

Anjali tried her best to be fair and just in determining all the issues while sorting out the complaints received—both false and real. With tempers running high, and her reputation in the process of being established, it was essential to not only *be* fair and transparent but to *appear* so too.

She spent hours scrutinizing the election material, reading at every opportunity even when only ten minutes were available. She read and re-read the election booklets on panchayat law and rules issued by the state authorities, and felt that every word was nearly stored in her memory.

Soon the day of the polls arrived. The SDM and the DSP left early by jeep to visit pre-identified trouble spots, and to check the preparedness of the police and revenue staff. They took a short break to refresh themselves with the tea and snacks thoughtfully packed by Mrs Bal. To pass the time, Gurpal recounted hair-raising experiences of quelling riots in the past—unintentionally raising Anjali's apprehensions about the day that had just begun.

They covered the polling booths in all the villages that had been identified as sensitive from the viewpoint of law and order, and visited as many other polling stations as they could. In some of them, the polling staff asked for clarifications about the law and the prescribed procedures.

Thanks to the number of times she had read the panchayat election manuals, Anjali was able to respond to their queries with clarity and conviction. The more seasoned officials were surprised that she could even address particularly tricky issues. She was able to assist the polling officers and respond to their queries about procedures with astuteness. The queries and discussions went a long way in her being accepted by the polling staff as a serious and responsible officer. Only she realized fully how theoretical her knowledge was.

As the day progressed, she gathered more confidence. It soon became apparent that the arrangements they had made over the last few weeks had been meticulous. Till the afternoon, calm prevailed, and it seemed that the polls were likely to be concluded without any untoward incident.

About an hour and a half before the polling was to be closed, the SDM and the DSP visited the polling station set up in a school in Bandewal—a large village located on the main highway. Bandewal was home to many unionized workers of a mill situated nearby, and had been identified as one of the most strife-ridden and sensitive villages in the subdivision. They had visited the place that morning when the polling process had just started. On this second visit, Anjali was pleased to find that the situation was as peaceful as it had been in the morning. There was friendly banter between the supporters of the two strong rival candidates, which was a source of amusement to people waiting to cast their votes. Reassured, they left for another village nearby.

Within fifteen minutes, a message was received on the police wireless system. Trouble was brewing in the Bandewal. A belligerent crowd had gathered outside the polling station. Worse, some people seemed to be carrying stones and bricks. The situation could turn serious. A small spark could set off an inferno in the politically sensitive environment. Both the SDM and the DSP knew that a violent incident in one district could reflect in other parts of the state, not just that day but also in the days to follow.

Turning their jeeps around, they reached the village post-haste. From a distance they could hear aggressive shouts even before they reached the polling station.

'This doesn't sound good, Bal Sahab,' Anjali said, trying to quell rising nervousness.

'No, madam. Both the candidates are politically strong. Their supporters are known to become violent at the drop of a hat. But we will handle it.'

'If there is violence, do we have enough force to handle it?'

DSP Bal shook his head slightly as he planned ahead.

The heated exchanges ceased as soon as the SDM and DSP entered the polling station. Two large groups stood near the raised corridor leading to the polling booth at the government school. Anjali was relieved to find that although the men looked angry, there was no sign of the dramatic battle she had feared. She and the DSP ascended the raised platform to talk to the two groups and to discover the problem.

'Madam ji, stones have been put into a ballot box by their men!' an angry voice reported.

'No, madam. We are a peace-loving group. We know about the sanctity of the ballot. None of us can even think of doing this. It is definitely someone from their side who has put stones in the ballot box!' said an older man with a grey flowing beard.

'DSP Sahab, you know us! Madam is new. We are winning. Why would we do anything to countermand the election?' shouted a burly man from the crowd.

'Nonsense! Your man is losing! That's why you resorted to such tricks,' said another from the opposite side.

The older man with the flowing beard, who had been a polling agent for many polls, folded his hands and spoke. 'Madam ji, the pebbles in the ballot box have vitiated the electoral process.'

'Yes!' Another person standing next to him supported him. 'The elections in our village have to be stayed.

'Indeed. We demand a re-poll. The ballot boxes have been desecrated!'

The air was filled with loud and angry voices contradicting each other and trying to outshout the other. Anjali noticed several men hiding pieces of broken bricks, picked up from a pile of construction material lying nearby, behind their backs. A few even held sticks torn off some trees in the compound.

'I need to be careful. This seems to be a situation that needs the gradual treatment the DSP had spoken about. I need to have my wits about me and appear in absolute control,' she thought to herself. She listened to the crowd with concentration. She knew it was important to give them an opportunity to vent their steam. 'Please speak one at a time so that I can hear everyone and understand what you are saying,' she said.

As she listened to the diatribe, she glanced at the pile of construction material lying near the rear wall. Here was more ammunition if a serious fight broke out. She was aware that there were a few police personnel waiting outside the polling station. They could be called in, but didn't seem adequate to control the large crowd. She had heard the DSP calling for reinforcements on the police wireless system, in case things got out of hand.

'But why should I allow things to go out of hand? There's no reason why we can't find an acceptable solution peacefully,' she thought as she heard both the groups out. She realized that the senior and more experienced DSP could have no legal response to the problem and was, in fact, looking to *her* for a solution.

The SDM's composure engaged the crowd's attention and helped soothe the charged atmosphere. Only Anjali knew how worried she was, despite her outward demeanour. Her mind raced to recollect all the rules she had read. She could remember none that dealt with stones-in-a-ballot-box.

Anjali remembered two administrative axioms from her training days: if the law and rules are silent on a given situation, use reason and common sense. Then find the rules or precedents to support your decision. Weighing the elements of the situation in her mind, it became clear to her that there was no case to stay the election. No one had been barred from voting, no ballot papers had been destroyed or tampered with, the seals on the ballot boxes were intact. It was only that inert material had been introduced into the cases. The stones would have to be small pebbles to be inserted through the narrow aperture of the boxes, and could not have damaged the ballots already inside.

Having come to this conclusion, Anjali decided that she wanted more certainty before announcing the decision. The consequences of a countermanded election were clear, but the aftermath of taking a poor decision would be disturbing.

She raised her hand in a restraining gesture with more confidence than she felt. Next, she asked her driver to bring her election booklets and texts of election laws and rules from the jeep. Then she stood apart from the crowd to consult the texts.

The horde, at first curious, began to grow impatient. The twenty-four-year-old RO of Gurdaspur was mortified that, for the first time during the poll, it was publicly visible that she did not have a ready answer. It did not help when she heard the DSP tell the crowd to calm down. 'Can't you see that SDM Sahiba is reading the law? Wait!'

She read through the familiar provisions again. Her decision was right, rational and reasoned, but there was no rule covering the problem at hand. She turned around to make the announcement and found the DSP right behind her. Very softly, Gurpal whispered what was becoming evident. 'One of the candidates seems to be losing badly. His supporters are in an ugly mood and want to cause trouble. They want the election countermanded.'

Anjali looked at the people standing behind the DSP. The crowd had begun to press forward to the platform. Some still looked curious about what the RO was doing. Many looked surly. The tension in the air could be cut with a knife.

Then Gurpal gave her a pragmatic suggestion—one only she could hear. 'Madam, please buy more time and continue to read your legal texts. The police force we have is insufficient to control this crowd. Our reinforcements will be here soon. It is best that you do not proclaim your verdict until they arrive.'

Anjali had already closed her books. She couldn't pretend to return to them. She temporized by stepping up to the edge of the podium and addressing the crowd in a raised voice. 'This is a very unusual situation. Never before has anyone put pebbles into a ballot box. I am looking for the proper legal solution to this problem and need to read the law a little longer. As the RO, I want to ensure that the decision I take is legally pucca (solid)—one that will be upheld in a court of law.'

Saying this she went back to poring over her books. Without missing a beat, Gurpal Bal, the DSP, took over. He spoke to the crowd in reasonable but firm tones and kept it engaged. Meanwhile, Anjali kept up the pretence of reading the legal provisions. She hoped that she conveyed the impression of an officer focused on seeking a solution based on law, and not of a novice out of her depth. Some of the men still looked searchingly at her and the legal texts in her hands. As she read, she heard comments about her manner of functioning from the crowd.

'This SDM is very legal minded. See how well she is reading the law!'

'She is new and this is her first election. Hopefully, she will be able to take a decision after careful deliberation.'

An older and more mature member agreed with the statement, and told the others that it was for their own benefit. 'See how hard she is working. Despite her young age, she is mature. Let us give the RO space and time to give the right decision based on the law. Let us not make any noise.'

Many of the men thought it was good that the RO was thorough, and weighing all the pros and cons. The women stood apart and watched. Another section of the mob was impatient, but didn't feel it right to interrupt an officer of the government reading the law. They were used to presiding officers in courts of law often stopping to look at their books.

After twenty minutes, Anjali saw police jeeps turning in from the school gates from the corner of her eye. With a sigh of relief, she stepped up to the edge of the platform to announce her decision. 'I have heard all the concerned parties, seen the locked ballot box in which a few pebbles have been inserted along with the ballot papers, and have also gone through the relevant legal provisions. The stones in the box cannot have damaged the votes. As the (RO) of Gurdaspur subdivision, I see no basis to countermand the elections of the village of Bandewal. I hereby declare that the polling process shall continue.'

The ruling was greeted with muted murmurs. A large part of the group was definitely hostile. Anjali wondered whether tempers were high enough for a riot to break out, regardless of the presence of a large police contingent. As she began to formulate a plan to handle that eventuality, she saw a major portion of the crowd melting away. In order to put distance between the newly arrived police force and themselves, many of them scaled the school's boundary wall.

'Isn't it surprising that so many villagers did not stay back to exercise their franchise?' the DSP asked a rhetorical question.

It was evident that there was more to the situation than met the eye. The troublemakers had run away.

Apparently, the entire crowd was not a part of the electorate of Bandewal.

'It seems many of them were outsiders who had come to foment trouble, in case the voting appeared to go against a particular candidate', said Gurpal, answering his own question.

The SDM and the DSP spent the next few minutes restarting the election process under police guard. Only after the poll resumed, and was running smoothly, did they leave Bandewal to continue their rounds of the remaining villages.

The entire process of rereading the law, and keeping the could-be-rioters engaged, had occupied all of twenty-five minutes. Somehow it seemed longer.

After all the votes had been cast by the electorate of 600 plus panchayats that day, they were stored in the ballot boxes and duly counted. The election results were announced, and Anjali breathed a sigh of satisfaction like the 'father of the bride'.

For the young SDM, the Bandewal episode was tough, albeit with a wealth of learning as a consequence. The massive respect she earned as the new SDM helped her handle larger challenges in the difficult times that the state was going through. The episode earned her the reputation of being a fair and just officer. Her reputation as an officer who took decisions as per the law in Bandewal gave Anjali a new label that brought a smile to her face: Kanooni Bibi!

Coda

The SDM sent a detailed report of the incident at Bandewal to the State Election Commissioner. Her decision was endorsed. The Bandewal episode upheld democracy and defeated a willful intent to cause affray and countermand the election.

The experience left Anjali wiser. She realized the value of remaining calm in potentially dangerous circumstances, as well as the power of listening. In time she learnt to look for patterns to identify hidden conflicting interests.

She developed the skills of defusing a situation with situation-specific tactics and confidence. While she remained posted in Gurdaspur, Anjali realized that the embarrassment of not having had a ready decision in Bandewal was outweighed by three distinct advantages: a riot was averted, the SDM and the DSP became a stronger team, and she gained a reputation for fairness, coming to be known as Kanooni Bibi.

X

Of Sensitive Sensibilities

Trade me not like merchandise . . .
I belong to none, and my body is mine . . .

'Oh my goodness, this little one can't be more than nine or ten! God alone knows how long she's been here. How did she come? And why on earth is she here?' Bhamathi saw the girl with large, bewildered eyes peeping at her from behind a door—a child who should have been at school and not in a brothel. A strong-willed officer, Bhamathi could not help but be moved by her plight. The eyes of the little girl, which hid so many dark and painful stories, continued to haunt her for days. A compassionate yet tough person, she possessed both sensitivity and courage necessary to help change the lives of unfortunate women who lived where many dreaded to tread—in the brothels of India.

Bhamathi's journey began in 1995 when she first saw a brothel. She was posted as the Executive Director (ED) of the Central Social Welfare Board (CSWB) under the Ministry of

Women and Child Development, Government of India. The CSWB had commissioned the Delhi School of Social Work to research prostitution. Pursuant to the research findings, she, as the ED, was required to prepare a road map for the future course of action. Earlier, she had implemented a few projects to address 'child prostitution', as it was called in those days. However, sitting in an office and working on a sensitive issue was entirely different from visiting the spot to see the conditions faced by the victims for herself. She was convinced that to make a proper impact, it was essential to meet them and understand what needed to be done.

A deep transformation took place in Bhamati's life the first day she visited a brothel in Delhi. She was both shocked and depressed at what she saw. The young ones looked bewildered, and said little, as she tried to interact with them. Some of the girls informed her that they were graduates and had been lured into the premises with the promise of a job. A few were clearly married and wore long mangalsutras—stringed black beads signifying their marital status. Bhamathi could not comprehend why they wanted to celebrate a marriage, which was, in fact, the very reason they were in the brothel.

She turned to a woman who said she was twenty-five, but looked haggard and had aged much before her time. 'You say your husband sold you to a human trafficker—and that is how you are here. So, why are you wearing a mangalsutra in the memory of the man who married you only to sell you off the next day?'

She received no answer except a resigned nod. An older woman responded on behalf of the young girl. 'What to do? That is our kismet . . .'

The strongest feeling in the cauldron of emotions Bhamathi's visit evoked in her was rage. She saw a large number of minor girls, who should have been at school but for the scourge of human trafficking. 'How can anyone put minor girls through this? Some of these young girls are mere children!' she thought. She could not sleep that night. What she had seen and heard that day kept playing on her mind. The visit that morning was a turning point in her life.

For a student of English literature, who cherished the works of Keats, Byron, Wordsworth and Coleridge, the visit to the brothel was horrific. The shattering experience brought home realities of a world she had not even been aware of. Her first few painful meetings with trafficked girls in 1995 set her on a life-altering path.

Bhamathi was determined to work for the cause of 'anti-human trafficking'. For her it was baptism by fire. She worked indomitably to make a difference, never looking back. On account of the exemplary work she did in the field of anti-human trafficking as the ED of the CSWB, she was posted as a Consultant at United Nations International Children's Emergency Fund (UNICEF)—where she helped bring out India's first 'Country Report on Child Prostitution'. The UNICEF country report was accepted by the Government of India, and several of its recommendations formed the agenda for the Central Advisory Board of the Ministry of Women and Child Development (MoWCD), under specific directives from the Supreme Court.

The Country Report on Child Prostitution flagged the issue of missing children and the 'culture of silence' that prevailed where the vulnerable had no voice. For the first time, the issue of missing children, and evidence-based link between child prostitution and missing children, were documented and projected in India.

The Country Report answered the question it asked: 'Where do they disappear?' Case studies concerning the follow-up of missing children, who were eventually rescued from places of exploitation like brothels and massage parlours, mostly located in other states, brought out the truth that the sociocultural devaluation of children, especially girls, was the major cause of vulnerability to human trafficking—and not mere poverty. The prime reason for child trafficking lay in the fact that a child's body was commoditized and was valued more as a product in a vile society.

The report titled 'The Silent Emergencies' was subtitled: 'I am a No(body), Just a (no)body!' The tag line of the country report was reminiscent of what a child in one of the brothels had said in answer to Bhamathi's questions:

'Where are you from? Who are your parents, dear? Where is your home? Tell me, child—who are you?'

The young girl had gazed into space and replied without looking at Bhamathi, 'I am nobody—just a nobody.'

Anti-human trafficking and rehabilitation of the victims became Bhamathi's mission. She made some important interventions wherever she was posted—whether in terms of policy, advocacy and capacity building in her UN assignments, or in hardcore policymaking ministries like the Ministry of Home Affairs.

When she served as Gender Adviser to the United Nations Population Fund (UNFPA), she carried forward the work she had done for anti-human trafficking in her capacity as

ED, CSWB, and as a Consultant with UNICEF. Given her experience, she brought special focus on sexual exploitation of vulnerable girls in the natal, marital and external world. Besides fighting female foeticide and infanticide, she helped provide policy inputs to prevent violence and crimes against women. Anti-human trafficking, as a broader and more holistic perspective on how women's bodies were treated, formed an integral part of the policy, operational and advocacy work.

On completion of her UNFPA assignment, Bhamathi was offered a permanent job with the organization. Around the same time, she received an exciting offer for a short-term assignment from the United Nations Development Programme (UNDP). She chose the latter, as the work was closer to her heart. As Senior Gender Adviser with the UNDP for South and Southeast Asia on mobility and HIV/AIDS, her role permitted her to pick up the threads and focus on anti–human trafficking again.

Bhamathi was responsible for the entire spectrum of safe mobility, migration, anti-trafficking initiatives, and vulnerability to HIV/AIDS in the region of India, Nepal, China, Pakistan, Japan, Korea and Thailand. Since unsafe migration was an area in which professional traffickers were prone to fish, she developed an anti–human trafficking strategy, which took into account the facts that trafficking, as a pattern of migration, removed migrants from the protection of their communities and from social support systems. Those caught in the web of trafficking had a lack of control over their working and living conditions, and their own bodies, and were more vulnerable to sexual exploitation, violence and

HIV/AIDS. Anti-trafficking and safe migration initiatives were undertaken against this contextual backdrop across the region.

A human-trafficking web portal was set up to prevent trafficking not only within India, but also across South and Southeast Asia, with a missing persons' page, fact sheets, database, and research and survey findings. A study established the baselines to form a Trafficked Survivors' Network for the region. Bhamathi helped to create anti-trafficking groups. This also helped to provide the much-needed linkages for isolated anti-trafficking groups across the area. Several interregional projects on unsafe mobility mainstreamed anti-trafficking in Nepal, India, China, Korea and Mongolia.

Bhamathi helped to develop and implement a Department for International Development (DFID) project called 'Prevention of Trafficking of Women and Girls and HIV/AIDS'. This DFID-funded project was accepted by the Government of India and implemented by the National Aids Control Organization (NACO) in partnership with the state governments. Capacity building of the judiciary, the police and the front-line institutions like NGOs and civil society organizations, was an integral part of the anti-human trafficking mission. Many trafficked victims volunteered as 'trainers' for the workshops. They were treated like all other consultants and subject experts, and their payments were on a par with theirs. Their participation enhanced the impact of the workshops.

The database on trafficking and HIV in the states of India provided the basis for policy interventions by the government. Standards of care to trafficked victims, and the provision of survival kits, were also an essential part of the project. Besides prevention, the ultimate goal was to support and reintegrate the trafficked victims into the society, overcoming stigma and discrimination.

Later, Bhamathi's work in the Ministry of Home Affairs in the Government of India, as Joint Secretary, and later Additional Secretary, for seven years, provided enough opportunity to her to work towards preventing human trafficking. By the time she joined, the United Nations Office on Drugs and Crime (UNODC), the global leader in the fight against drugs and crime, had funded the setting up a few Anti-Human Trafficking Units (AHTUs), and some had been already been set up as a pilot project, before she joined MHA. Bhamathi, seeing the efficacy of the pilot project, helped to upscale and institutionalize the AHTUs across India, with innovative ideas.

The Planning Commission and the Finance Department did not allocate the requisite funds for Bhamathi's proposal for 330 AHTUs, pointing out that the MHA had no role to play in anti-human trafficking, as it was the mandate of the Ministry of Women and Child Development as per the rules of business. Moreover, crime was a state subject.

Bhamathi came up with an innovative solution. She posed the problem and obtained approval for setting up AHTUs across the country with the Home Minister's approval under the Police Modernization Scheme—which continues to fund the AHTUs from the same head of accounts. Nodal officers were appointed by the state governments to monitor them closely. Experts and NGOs were invited to familiarize the nodal officers with the strategies in dealing with the crime from a rights and gender-sensitive perspective. Trafficked survivors were also invited to address the officers of AHTUs for a closer understanding of the problem. Over the years, the MHA AHTUs have become firmly embedded in the law-enforcement framework of the country.

The annual data published by the Bureau of Police Research and Development (BPRD) records statistics that have shown an improvement in identified performance indicators after the setting up of the AHTUs. An AHTU is a well-recognized specialized body to investigate trafficking-related crimes, and is the mainstay of India's fight against human trafficking.

During the seven years that Bhamathi worked in the MHA, the ministry became the national platform for the fight against the crime of human trafficking with cooperation from all the concerned ministries, including the Ministry of Labour, and of Women and Child Development. The active involvement of the MHA gave a more focused push for the enforcement of existing provisions of the law to stop human trafficking. Efforts across the country improved: rescue operations of minors, apprehension of traffickers, investigations into organized crimes, conviction of offenders, rehabilitation of victims, closure of brothels, non-victimization of victims, and attempts at expediting the repatriation of foreigners. The Crime and Criminal Tracking Network Systems (CCTNS) that connects the entire country, has a special software module to track missing children.

Capacity-building programmes across the country were institutionalized by the BPRD. The training modules, curricula, methodology, training aids, resource materials and evaluation format, were institutionalized along the lines of the methodologies developed by Bhamathi at the UNFPA and the UNDP earlier. Senior officers of the Central Bureau of Investigation (CBI) were trained to deal with human trafficking from the perspective of organized-crime. An AHTU was also set up at the CBI. The Border Security Force, Indo Tibetan Border Police and Seema Suraksha Bal, on the Indo-Nepal border, were sensitized and oriented to cross-border human trafficking.

Capacity building of the third important wing of criminal justice administration, the judiciary, was also institutionalized after a national consultation in partnership with the Ministry of Law and Justice, Government of India. Bhamathi took various steps to enhance the awareness of the community, including through virtual and distance learning. One such initiative was a certificate course on Anti-Human Trafficking launched by the Home Minister at the Indira Gandhi National Open University (IGNOU). The course was extended to all the countries in the South Asian Association for Regional Cooperation (SAARC) region.

Bhamathi issued a revolutionary advisory for women and children, who had been languishing in Indian jails for several years. This had far-reaching consequences, and brought about a major change in dealing with rescued victims who were foreign nationals. The advisory directed that a foreign national trafficked from across the border would not be prosecuted in India for the violation of the passport and visa regime, once it was confirmed that the person was a victim of human trafficking. This heralded a new system of expeditious repatriation of the victims of transborder trafficking.

Earlier, several foreign victims of human trafficking were not only arrested and prosecuted, but often convicted for violation of the visa-and-passport regime. They languished in jails and shelters of state governments for years—mostly as illegal migrants.

Systems were put in place. A committee of officers from the MHA, External Affairs and Women and Child Development, was constituted, that reached out to the embassies and high commissions to assist the foreign nationals trapped in the jails. In the very first year, 253 trafficked Bangladeshi victims, who had been in prisons or shelters for several years, were assisted to return home.

The years Bhamathi spent in the CSWB, and on the various United Nation assignments—including UNICEF, the UNFPA and the UNDP—were loci along a path of a war against the scourge of human trafficking, which culminated in a huge gain at the MHA. This was a period of consolidation of the efforts she had undertaken so far—a period that witnessed the integration of policy and programme. The MHA years showed a wonderful convergence of advocacy, planning, policy and action. Challenges became opportunities, which threw up innovative advances towards a silent revolution—a revolution that Bhamathi hoped would one day ensure that no young child would ever turn back and say with sad vacant eyes: 'I am a nobody . . . a no body . . .'

Coda

Bhamathi is a recipient of the Exemplary Lifetime Commitment Award for Work on Anti-Human Trafficking and is now retired.

She lives in Chennai. Her mission, anti-human trafficking, continues. After superannuation, she is still invited as an expert to various international seminars and conferences on human trafficking, women's empowerment, the safety of children online/on digital platforms, and the empowerment of adolescents.

Bhamathi has set up a Trust called ASSET to support victims of trafficking. She has authored and published several articles on the subject, including one on 'Cybercrimes against Women and Children'.

She always found room for anti-human trafficking in whichever area she worked. After the MHA, she worked as the Financial Adviser in the Ministry of Rural Development, and made efforts to mainstream anti-trafficking in the ministry's sustainable livelihood programmes. The victims of human trafficking, upon return to their homes, needed reintegration and non-stigmatization. Several states undertook stand-alone projects for trafficked victims and their rehabilitation.

Bhamathi's award citation reads: 'Your persistent efforts have really inspired all of us in civil society to continue the fight against this crime against humanity. We recognize the inspiring and hard work done by you, which has inspired hundreds of anti-trafficking activists across the country.'

Acknowledgements

Women of Influence is a combined effort of many people, whose contributions I would like to acknowledge with gratitude. The idea of the book came from my daughter, Lakshi, a few days after the lockdown was announced during the Covid pandemic in March 2020. We were watching a rather acrimonious debate on television, and yet another episode of 'Bash the Babu' was playing, with all the screeching and screaming. The IAS has always been a favourite whipping boy!

All through my career of about three-and-a-half decades, I have maintained stoic silence. Perhaps I am of the old school. My conviction that the truth ultimately prevails has always been vindicated, though sometimes with a little delay. My children have walked the tumultuous path with me, and witnessed the trials and tribulations at close quarters. The acidic comments about babus and babudom have little connection with what they have seen and experienced. My daughter wondered why the narrative was not corrected by a truer picture, and suggested that I should write about my own journey. Being rather reserved myself, I did the next best thing. I did some research, asked around, spoke to a few outstanding officers over the phone—and began writing the book, *Women of Influence*.

I have worked closely with some of the protagonists, seen and admired the work of others from a distance, and heard and read about a few I couldn't meet but interacted with over the phone.

For their extremely valuable contributions to the book, I would like to thank:

Ms Otima Bordia, Ms Anuradha Gupta, the late Ms Anita Kaul, Dr Maitreyi Bordia Das, Dr Malini Shankar, Ms Durga Shakti Nagpal, Dr Anita Chowdhary, Ms Shakuntala Doley Gamlin, Ms Anjuly Chib Duggal, and Ms B. Bhamathi.

I would also like to extend my gratitude to Sanjay Kaul and Rohan Kaul, for helping me understand Anita Kaul better, and for providing information on some vital and interesting personal elements in her journey. I would also like to express my gratitude to Ms. Maitreyi Bordia Das, who spent several long evenings sharing details of her mother's story from memory over some rather long long-distance calls from Washington. Since Ms Otima Bordia was not well enough to talk to me directly, her daughter Maitreyi shared some of her recorded messages over the phone. It was a pleasure hearing about the events and her experiences first hand in Otima Bordia's voice.

This book—our book—is my token of respect and regard for all the women of substance presented here and the values they stood for.